SHREDDED COOKBOOK

101 Delicious, Fast, High Protein Recipes

**Gluten Free
High Protein
30 Min
or Less**

Mike Kneuer

CPT, CES, FNS, FAS, Professional Physique Athlete
Mike@IronForkFitness.com

Mike Kneuer is a personal trainer and professional physique athlete in Boca Raton, FL. Mike is passionate about health and fitness and helping others make positive life changes. He has been working in the fitness industry for over a decade and specializes in helping his fitness family reach their goals through nutrition and exercise programming.

In order to help his clients see that eating healthy isn't difficult, time-consuming or boring, Mike posts a photograph of everything that he eats online at www. WhatMikeEats.com, also on Instagram and Twitter @WhatMikeEats. By using social media, Mike has helped thousands of people around the world change the way they think about eating healthy foods and helped them reach their fitness goals

Mike's passion for nutrition and healthy eating led him to create this cookbook, including some of his favorite recipes, proving it is possible to make fast, great tasting healthy meals.

If you would like to work with Mike please email him at
Mike@IronForkFitness.com

The Standard American Diet is SAD

The nutrition of most Americans is pretty S.A.D. The Standard American Diet is loaded with processed foods and "food-like products" that are high in refined carbs, sugars, and chemicals. It's practically devoid of any vegetables and fruits. Most meats and dairy products are full of hormones and antibiotics. It's a SAD state of affairs. Just go take a stroll through your nearest mall, grocery store, or even better your local Wal-Mart and you will get a clear picture of the average American, their diet (just look in their cart), and their body type (hint: It's OVERWEIGHT). We are at a point in our country where 2/3 of the population is overweight. Yes, you read that right–overweight has become the norm. Scary, right?

Why is this happening? Our grocery stores are loaded with highly processed crap that's full of sugar. In fact, over 80% of products on the shelves in your grocery store have added sugar. Combine that with the FDA's ridiculous recommendations for a low-fat and high-carb diet in the 1950's and that's a recipe for disaster,(pun intended). It's no wonder the obesity and diabetes rates have skyrocketed since the 1950's. People used to eat real food. When your grandma or great grandma was your age most of the products you eat did not even exist.

Add to this nutritional shit storm all of the fad diets, so called nutrition experts, and food companies with huge marketing budget and lobbyists in Washington and the problem compounds exponentially. There is so much blatant misinformation out there about food and what's healthy. Every week there is a new magazine with "The Best Diet Ever" or some crazy unsustainable "Cookie Diet". Have you heard of that one? It's a real thing. I know, I was dumbfounded when I heard of this, but there is a ridiculous diet that suggests you only eat cookies from a particular company and they promise you will lose weight. How is that supposed to fulfill your nutritional requirements? And how long can you actually eat cookies for every day? Please.

But people are desperate for help and people are inherently lazy. So they want a quick fix, which doesn't work when it comes to your health. There is no magic pill, potion, or diet cookie that is going to save the world from obesity. It's not rocket science, it's simply making informed decisions based on facts. Think about food like fuel for your body (you wouldn't put 83 octane in a Ferrari so why fuel your body with crap?)

Time has also become an issue as everyone is so busy rushing around that often times meals are either handed to you through your car window or come in the form of a pre-packaged microwavable nonsense.

This is where the Shredded Chef Cookbook comes in to save the day....

This book was designed to eliminate the excuse of time and difficulty out of making healthy meals. Each one of these delicious recipes is prepared and cooked in 30 minutes or less and is nutritious and free of any unhealthy ingredients (we'll get to the list in a little bit).

The Shredded Chef Cookbook is a collection of my favorite healthy recipes that have been made healthier, higher in protein, and faster to cook. All of the recipes are gluten free, soy free, no added sugar, and no artificial BS....just real, healthy, and delicious ingredients that support optimal health and body composition.

It's time to take our health back and it starts in the kitchen!

Cooking Made Quick and Easy

The recipes in this cookbook are all fast and easy to cook and you don't need to be a professional chef to make them. You now have 101 options for a healthy meal that takes less time to make than to watch your favorite sitcom.

High Protein Meals

Every recipe in the Shredded Chef Cookbook has been designed to have at least 30g protein per serving. Protein is important for supporting lean muscle and also helps you feel full longer due to its satiety. This means you'll feel great, won't be hungry, and have the body you want (of course combined with exercise).

Banned Ingredients

The following ingredients are unhealthy and do not support optimal health. In order to make the Shredded Chef Cookbook the healthiest possible each of the recipes I've collected have been modified to not contain any of the following:

- Processed Foods – most processed foods are stripped of their nutrients, fortified with synthetic vitamins, and loaded with sodium, sugar, or artificial ingredients.
- Sugar – Create inflammation, spikes insulin levels, creates addiction, makes you fat.
- Soy - Mostly GMO and can raise estrogen levels (that's bad) and has compounds that rob your body of important minerals.
- Artificial Sweeteners – disrupt endocrine (hormone) system, linked to various cancers, changes micro biome (bacteria) in gut leading to glucose intolerance
- Sodium Nitrates – Primarily found in processed meats; these chemicals have been linked to cancer.
- Artificial Colors – these are petroleum based and have been linked to numerous health problems.
- Gluten- Gluten is in wheat, barley, and rye. Wheat or some form of wheat is in a large majority of the foods in the supermarket. It's also in most flours, breads, crackers, and packaged carbohydrates. It can be found in everything from shampoo to salad dressing. I'm not recommending that you eat gluten free shampoo; I'm highlighting the scope of its penetration into our daily lives. Gluten has been linked to many health problems. It's estimated that only 1% of the population has Celiac disease, which means they cannot have ANY gluten whatsoever. Approximately 10% (I personally think it's higher) have sensitivities to gluten. The problem I have with gluten is that most of the crappy processed food-like products we aren't supposed to be eating have gluten in them. Let's run down a quick list: cake, cookies, pretzels, cereals, breads, pasta, and almost anything that comes packaged in a box. These are the foods that we need to stay away from regardless of gluten to get shredded. These are crappy carbs and will not result in a 6 pack.

- **MSG or Monosodium Glutamate**

MSG is a neurotoxin that apparently tastes pretty good because it is added to a lot of foods. Remember the big Chinese food MSG controversy? Well it's not just in Chinese food. It's in a huge array of processed foods. Its also hidden under some sneaky names like yeast extract, hydrolyzed anything, autolyzed anything, and the worst "natural flavor". Not all "Natural Flavor" is MSG but you really have no clue what it is unless you contact the manufacturer directly. This link should help clarify any MSG questions: http://www.msgtruth.org/avoid.htm

I really hope you enjoy these healthy recipes I have compiled and improved over the years and THANK YOU again for your purchase of the Shredded Chef Cookbook.

If you are looking for help reaching your health and fitness goals please feel free to contact me. I work with people all over the country to get healthier, look better, and feel their best. I'd love to have you as part of my Fitness Family.

In Health,

Mike Kneuer – CPT, CES, FNS, FAS, Pro Physique Athlete

Connect with Mike

Mike@ProjectShredded.com

Facebook.com/MikeKneuer82

Instagram.com/WhatMikeEats

Twitter.com/WhatMikeEats

Linkedin.com/in/MikeKneuer

Youtube.com/c/MikeKneuer82

Google.com/+MikeKneuer82

click on recipe link to page

CONTENTS

click on recipe link to page

CHICKEN

SEAFOOD

SALMON

103. Spinach Salad with Salmon Nectarines and Pecans

104. Wild Salmon Curry With Tomatoes

105. Salmon With Mint Dressing

106. Lemon Sriracha Salmon

SHRIMP

107. Roasted Spaghetti Squash With Garlic Shrimp

109. Asian Pepper Shrimp With Cilantro

110. Cheesy Shrimps And Grits

111. Curried Shrimp With Sugar Snap Peas

112. Spicy Grilled Shrimp

113. Lemon Pepper Shrimp

TUNA

114. Tuna Salad

115. Tuna, Fennel And Bean Salad

116. Tuna And Parsley Pesto Sauce

117. Pan Seared Tuna Steaks

118. Tuna Steaks Moroccan-Style

119. Tuna And Lemon Pasta

MISCELLANEOUS SEAFOOD

120. Steamed Mussels

121. Asian Flounder Fillet

122. Poached Bass Over Frisee Salad

123. Mahi-Mahi With Macadamia Nut Crust

124. Grilled Mahi-Mahi With Spicy Carribean Sauce

125. Sesame Seed Crusted Snapper

Oatmeal Bowl

SERVINGS: 1 BOWL   PREP TIME: 2 MINUTES   COOK TIME: 3 MINUTES

Nutritional Facts

Calories	Protein	Fat	Carbs	Dietary Fiber	Sugar
475	30g	16g	57g	20g	15g

Note: Nutrition information does not include ingredients for garnish.

INGREDIENTS

½ medium ripe banana, mashed

2 tbsp chia seeds

1/3 cup rolled oats

1/3 tsp ground cinnamon

2/3 cup almond milk or cashew milk

1/3 cup water

1 scoop of Life Time Fitness Grass Fed Whey Protein Chocolate

1 tbsp ground flax seeds

Garnish

Soaked almonds

Hemp hearts

Ground cinnamon

Toasted coconut

Almond butter

INSTRUCTIONS

1. The night before, prepare and combine mashed bananas, chia seeds, oatmeal, ground cinnamon, milk and water in a large bowl. Mix well until combined.

2. Cover and refrigerate overnight.

3. Place oatmeal mixture into a pan the next morning. Bring mixture to a simmer, stirring frequently until it has thickened. Lastly, add ground flax seeds at the end of cooking time.

4. Place oats in a bowl and garnish with your favorite toppings.

5. Eat, Enjoy and Be Healthy!

Cottage Cheese
Omelet with Veggies

SERVINGS: 2 PREP TIME: 3 MINUTES COOK TIME: 5 MINUTES

Nutritional Facts

Calories	Protein	Fat	Carbs	Dietary Fiber	Sugar
357	35g	20g	7g	1g	3g

Note: Nutrition information does not include ingredients for garnish.

INGREDIENTS

1 ½ cups of eggs, beaten (about 5 eggs)

¾ cup cottage cheese (2%)

¼ cup sweet onions, chopped

1 cup fresh spinach

6 pieces cherry tomatoes, diced

Cooking oil spray

INSTRUCTIONS

1. Spray skillet with a generous amount of cooking oil spray over medium-high heat.

2. When oil is hot, add beaten eggs and chopped onions.

3. Fry as you would to the traditional omelet. When the bottom of omelet is slightly golden, add 1/5 of the cottage cheese, ½ cup of spinach and chopped tomatoes on half part of the omelet.

4. Cook the omelet for about 2 minutes until the fillings are hot, then flip the bare half of the omelet into the full side to make a perfect half circle.

5. Gently slide the omelet into a serving plate, top with remaining cottage cheese.

6. Eat, Enjoy and Be Healthy!

Power
Protein Crepes

Nutritional Facts

Calories	Protein	Fat	Carbs	Dietary Fiber	Sugar
238	42g	0g	6g	1g	1g

INGREDIENTS

4 large egg whites

1 scoop protein powder (Life Time Fitness – VeganMax)

Water (a splash)

½ cup Greek yogurt (for extra protein)

INSTRUCTIONS

1. In a bowl, combine protein powder with a splash of water. Stir in egg whites.

2. Heat a non-stick skillet over medium heat, then pour 1/3 of the batter. Cook until small bubbles form.

3. Flip to cook the other side, about 10 seconds. Repeat the process with the remaining batter.

4. Fill with fresh blueberries and top with Greek yogurt

5. Eat, Enjoy and Be Healthy!

Triple
Berry Oatmeal

SERVINGS: 1   PREP TIME: 2 MINUTES

Nutritional Facts

Calories	Protein	Fat	Carbs	Dietary Fiber	Sugar
630	50g	27g	45g	4g	13g

INGREDIENTS

1/3 cup rolled oats

1 cup Greek-style yogurt

½ cup mixed berries

1 scoop vanilla whey protein powder

INSTRUCTIONS

1.   Cook rolled oats according to package directions.

2.   Stir in yogurt, berries and protein powder.

3.   Eat, Enjoy and Be Healthy!

Greek Quinoa Omelets With
Feta and Tzatziki

SERVINGS: 3   PREP TIME: 15 MINUTES   COOK TIME: 10 MINUTES

Nutritional Facts

Calories	Protein	Fat	Carbs	Dietary Fiber	Sugar
815	37g	53g	47g	7g	11.5g

INGREDIENTS

Tzatziki

1 cup plain Greek yogurt

¼ cucumber, peeled, seeded and diced small

1 large clove garlic, minced

½ tbsp white wine vinegar

½ tsp dried dill

1 tsp dried oregano

1 tbsp fresh lemon juice

1 tbsp extra virgin olive oil

Omelets

6 large eggs

¼ cup milk

2 tbsp butter, divided

1 ½ cup quinoa, cooked

1 cup fresh spinach, chopped

½ cup pitted kalamata olives, halved

1 tbsp olive brine

¼ cup roasted red peppers, chopped or sliced

¼ cup marinated artichoke hearts, chopped

¼ cup oil packed sundried tomatoes

1 tbsp sundried tomato oil

2 cloves garlic, minced or grated

1 tsp dried oregano

1 tsp dried basil

Himalayan Pink salt

Ground black pepper, to taste

2 oz feta cheese, crumbled

¼ cup toasted pine nuts, for topping

Fresh grape tomatoes, for topping

1 avocado, sliced, for topping

Please See Next Page

INSTRUCTIONS

1. In a large bowl, combine yogurt (must be thick), diced cucumber garlic, white wine vinegar, dill, oregano, and lemon juice. Season with salt and pepper.

2. Drizzle olive oil over the mixture. Refrigerate for at least 30 minutes.

3. In another large bowl, combine cooked quinoa, chopped spinach, olives, roasted red peppers, chopped artichokes, sun-dried tomatoes, garlic, oregano and basil.

4. Add 1 tbsp of oil from the sundried tomatoes and 1 tbsp of olive brine. Season with salt and pepper. Toss well and set aside.

5. To prepare the omelet, whisk eggs, milk and a dash of salt and pepper in a large bowl.

6. Heat skillet over medium heat, then add 1 tbsp of butter. Swirl skillet to coat the bottom and sides with melted butter.

7. Pour half of the egg mixture into the skillet and cook for about 10 to 20 seconds.

8. Sprinkle the omelet with some feta or shredded mozzarella cheese.

9. Place cooked omelet onto a plate.

10. Sprinkle the omelet with some feta cheese, then fill with quinoa salad. Fold over and keep warm. Repeat the process with the remaining omelet.

11. Serve omelet with Tzatziki, feta cheese and grape tomatoes. Garnish with avocado slices.

12. Eat, Enjoy and Be Healthy!

Egg White Omelet With
Mushroom, Ham & Cheese

SERVINGS: 2   PREP TIME: 5 MINUTES   COOK TIME: 5 MINUTES

Nutritional Facts

Calories	Protein	Fat	Carbs	Dietary Fiber	Sugar
320	30.5g	17g	9g	1.5g	3g

INGREDIENTS

8 large egg whites

3 slices extra-lean chopped ham

2 2/3 slices Swiss cheese (low fat)

1 cup mushrooms, chopped

Coconut oil cooking spray

INSTRUCTIONS

1. Heat a skillet over medium heat. Spray with cooking oil spray.

2. In a large bowl, whisk together egg whites, ham, cheese and mushrooms,

3. Cook omelet until set.

4. Eat, Enjoy and Be Healthy!

High Protein
Pancakes

SERVINGS: 1 PREP TIME: 5 MINUTES COOK TIME: 10 MINUTES

Nutritional Facts

Calories	Protein	Fat	Carbs	Dietary Fiber	Sugar
585	40g	36g	24g	19g	1g

INGREDIENTS

3 eggs

¼ cup freshly ground flax seed

½ cup ricotta cheese (skim)

1 tsp baking powder

½ tsp salt

INSTRUCTIONS

1. In a bowl, combine all ingredients and mix it well to achieved a smooth batter.

2. Heat a griddle or non-stick skillet over medium high heat and spray with cooking oil spray.

3. Spoon pancake mixture into a skillet and shape into round pancakes.

4. Cook for about 2 minutes on each side or until slightly browned.

5. Serve pancakes with butter and low-carb syrup, sour cream or berries.

6. Eat, Enjoy and Be Healthy!

Asian Mushu Steak Wraps

SERVINGS: 3   COOK TIME: 25-30 MINUTES

Nutritional Facts

Calories	Protein	Fat	Carbs	Dietary Fiber	Sugar
510	37g	16g	53g	12g	19g

INGREDIENTS

4 pieces tri-tip beef steaks (grass fed), about 4 oz each

¾ tsp ground cinnamon

¼ tsp ground black pepper

¼ cup Hoisin sauce

1 tbsp honey

Himalayan pink salt

3 cups tri-color coleslaw mix (green cabbage, red cabbage and carrots)

1 Granny Smith apple, cored and thinly sliced

8 medium tortillas (gluten free), warmed

INSTRUCTIONS

1. Season beef steaks with cinnamon and ground black pepper.

2. Heat a non-stick skillet over medium high heat. Cook steak for about for about 12 minutes, turning occasionally.

3. Transfer cooked steak in a plate and let rest for 5 minutes. Carve steaks into thin slices, then season with a dash of salt and pepper.

4. In a large bowl, combine honey and Hoisin sauce. Mix well. Add in steak slices, coleslaw mix and apple slices. Toss gently to combine.

5. Divide beef mixture on each tortilla, leaving 1 ½-inch border on each side.

6. Fold tortilla, bottom edge up over filling. Fold right and left side to center, overlapping edges and secure with a wooden toothpick.

7. Eat, Enjoy and Be Healthy!

Bacon Burger

SERVINGS: 4   PREP TIME: 20 MINUTES

Nutritional Facts

Calories	Protein	Fat	Carbs	Dietary Fiber	Sugar
715	47g	36g	50g	4g	7g

INGREDIENTS

2 ½ tsp olive oil

1 ½ lbs ground beef (grass fed)

4 slices nitrate free bacon, chopped

4 pieces gluten free English muffin, split

4 large eggs

1 large tomato, sliced

Himalayan pink salt, to taste

Ground black pepper

INSTRUCTIONS

1. Heat grill to medium high heat. Oil the grill grate just before grilling time.

2. Meanwhile, combine ground beef, bacon, ½ tsp salt and ½ tsp ground black pepper.

3. Shape ground beef mixture into ¾-inch thick patties. Using your finger, make a shallow indentation on top of each patty to prevent over-plumping during cooking time.

4. Grill beef patties for about 4 minutes on each side for medium rare.

5. Meanwhile, grill English muffins skin-side down until toasted.

6. Heat oil in a large skillet. Add eggs and cook, covered for about 3 minutes for a slightly runny yolk. Season with a dash of salt and pepper.

7. Fill each muffins with beef patty, egg and slice of tomato.

8. Eat, Enjoy and Be Healthy!

Beef And
Bean Chile Verde

SERVINGS: 4   COOK TIME: 30 MINUTES

Nutritional Facts

Calories	Protein	Fat	Carbs	Dietary Fiber	Sugar
310	32g	10g	22g	6g	5g

INGREDIENTS

1 lb lean ground beef (grass fed)

1 large red bell pepper, chopped

1 large onion, chopped

6 cloves garlic, chopped

1 tbsp chili powder

2 tsp ground cumin

¼ tsp cayenne pepper, or to taste

1 (16-oz) jar green salsa, green enchilada sauce or taco sauce

¼ cup water

1 (15-oz) can pinto or kidney beans, rinsed

INSTRUCTIONS

1. Heat a large saucepan over medium heat. When hot, place beef, bell pepper and onion and cook until for about 8 to 10 minutes or until the meat is brown.

2. Stir in garlic, chili powder, cumin and cayenne. Sauté for about 15 seconds or until aromatic.

3. Pour in salsa (or sauce) and water, lower the heat and cook covered until the vegetables are tender, 10 to 15 minutes. Stir from time to time.

4. Add beans and cook for 1 more minute or until the beans are heated through.

5. Eat, Enjoy and Be Healthy!

Beef
Ragu
Zoodles

SERVINGS: 4 COOK TIME: 25 minutes

Nutritional Facts

Calories	Protein	Fat	Carbs	Dietary Fiber	Sugar
610	49g	40g	11g	3g	3g

INGREDIENTS

Beef Ragu

2 lbs grass fed ground beef (thaw if frozen)

½ cup red pesto

1 tbsp ghee or grass fed butter

1 bunch fresh parsley

½ tsp Himalayan pink salt

Zoodles

4 medium fresh zucchini

INSTRUCTIONS

1. Melt half of ghee or butter in a saucepan over medium high heat. Add ground beef and sauté until brown, stirring frequently about 5 to 8 minutes.

2. Add red pesto and fresh chopped parsley. Turn the heat to low and cook for at least 2 minutes. Turn off the heat and pour ground beef mixture into a bowl.

3. Prepare the zucchini by creating zucchini noodles using spiralizer. Alternatively, use a julienne peeler and peel zucchini all around until to the soft core.

4. Heat remaining ghee or butter into a saucepan and add zoodles (zucchini noodles). Stir-fry for 2-3 minutes or until al dente. Do not overcook. Turn off the heat.

5. Combine cooked zoodles with the ground beef mixture. Mix gently.

6. Eat, Enjoy and Be Healthy!

Stir-Fried
Beef and Ginger

SERVINGS: 4 PREP TIME: 5 MINUTES COOK TIME: 25 MINUTES

Nutritional Facts

Calories	Protein	Fat	Carbs	Dietary Fiber	Sugar
475	41.5g	18g	35g	5g	0g

INGREDIENTS

Marinade

1/3 cup coconut aminos

½ cup chicken broth

3 tbsp rice wine vinegar

2 tbsp cornstarch

2 tsp ground ginger

¼ tsp freshly ground
 black pepper

Stir-Fry Ingredients

1 lb grass fed flank steak or beef sirloin,
sliced into thin strips

2 garlic cloves, minced

2 tbsp olive oil

8 oz baby Portobello mushrooms, halved

3 cups kale, chopped

2 stalks green onion, thinly sliced

INSTRUCTIONS

1. Prepare the marinade by combining all ingredients in a bowl. Whisk to combine, then transfer the marinade into a Ziploc bag.

2. Place flank steak or sirloin inside and massage gently with the marinade.

3. Seal the bag and refrigerate for 15 minutes.

4. When ready to stir-fry, heat 1 tbsp of oil in a large skillet or sauté pan over medium-high heat. Add Marinated steak and garlic, reserving the marinade for later use.

5. Sauté for about 3 minutes or until steak and garlic browns slightly, stirring frequently.

6. Transfer steak on a platter and set aside.

7. To the same skillet, add mushrooms, kale and reserved marinade. Cook until kale is wilted, the mushrooms are soft and the sauce has reduced and has thickened.

8. Add in steak and mix gently to combine.

9. Serve over plain white rice or quinoa with a sprinkling of chopped green onions on top.

10. Eat, Enjoy and Be Healthy!

Spicy Beef And
Sweet Potatoes with Crispy Eggs

SERVINGS: 4   PREP TIME: 10 MINUTES   COOK TIME: 15 MINUTES

Nutritional Facts

Calories	Protein	Fat	Carbs	Dietary Fiber	Sugar
725	36g	59g	10.5	2g	3g

INGREDIENTS

Spiced beef and sweet potatoes

2 sweet potatoes, peeled and finely chopped

Olive oil and/or butter

1 lb ground beef

2 shallots, halved and sliced

1 tsp ground coriander

½ tsp ground turmeric

¼ tsp ground cardamom

1/8 tsp ground allspice

Himalayan pink salt, to taste

Ground black pepper, to taste

Crispy eggs

Olive or avocado oil

4 large eggs

Salt, to taste

Ground black pepper, to taste

Please See Next Page

INSTRUCTIONS

1. Placed chopped sweet potatoes in a microwave safe bowl with 3 tbsp of water. Cover and microwave on High for 3 minutes or until sweet potatoes are firm but can easily pierced with a fork. Drain.

2. Heat oil in a large skillet over medium heat. Add ground beef and cook until browned.

3. Stir in the shallots, spices, salt, and fresh ground pepper.

4. Add the pre-cooked sweet potatoes and increase the heat.

5. Cook until the sweet potatoes are soft and slightly golden. Season to taste. Remove from heat, cover and keep warm.

6. Meanwhile, to make the crispy eggs, heat a large heavy bottomed skillet over medium heat for 1 minute. Add a generous amount of oil.

7. Crack in the eggs and cook until whites are set on the bottom and browned around the edges. Continue to cook and baste until the eggs are cooked to your liking.

8. Divide beef and sweet potatoes over four bowls.

9. Place an egg on top of each bowl. Season with salt and pepper and serve hot.

10. Eat, Enjoy and Be Healthy!

Asian
Lettuce Wraps

SERVINGS: 2   PREP TIME: 15 MINUTES   COOK TIME: 15 MINUTES

Nutritional Facts

Calories	Protein	Fat	Carbs	Dietary Fiber	Sugar
385	50g	16.5g	8.5g	3.5g	5g

INGREDIENTS

2 tbsp coconut aminos

12 lettuce leaves

1 tbsp garlic powder

1 lb lean ground beef (grass fed)

INSTRUCTIONS

1. Combine coconut aminos and garlic powder in a small bowl. Whisk to combine.

2. Pour marinade mixture over ground beef. Mix well. Set aside for 1 hour.

3. Heat the skillet over medium heat. Brown marinated ground beef.

4. Serve ground beef with lettuce leaves.

5. Eat, Enjoy and Be Healthy.

Steak With
Mushrooms & Asparagus

SERVINGS: 4 PREP TIME: 15 MINUTES   COOK TIME: 15 MINUTES

Nutritional Facts

Calories	Protein	Fat	Carbs	Dietary Fiber	Sugar
360	42g	16.5g	11g	4g	5g

INGREDIENTS

1 ½ lbs London broil beef steak (1-inch thick)

4 cloves garlic, minced

4 tsp rosemary, crushed

2 tbsp extra virgin olive oil

1 small onion

1 lb asparagus, cut into 2-inch pieces

1 lb white mushrooms, sliced

1 tbsp lemon zest

INSTRUCTIONS

1. Make a diamond pattern on both sides of steak by carefully making 1/8-inch deep diagonal cuts with 1-inch intervals.

2. Season steak with half of minced garlic and 2 tsp of crushed rosemary on both sides. Sprinkle with salt and ground pepper.

3. Heat 1 tbsp of oil in a large skillet over medium heat.

4. Cook steak for about 4 minutes per side (for medium rare). Cook steak to your desired doneness.

5. Transfer steak to a plate and cover with foil to keep warm.

6. Heat remaining oil in the same skillet. Sauté onion for 2 minutes.

7. Stir in remaining garlic and sauté with the onion until fragrant.

8. Stir in mushrooms and asparagus. Cook, stirring frequently until asparagus is crisp and tender and all the liquid has evaporated, about 5 minutes.

9. Stir in lemon zest and remaining rosemary. Season to taste with salt and pepper.

10. Slice the steak thinly and serve with the cooked vegetables.

11. Eat, Enjoy and Be Healthy!

Steak With Shallots & Sauteed Watercress

SERVINGS: 4   COOK TIME: 30 MINUTES

Nutritional Facts

Calories	Protein	Fat	Carbs	Dietary Fiber	Sugar
555	42.5g	41g	4g	1g	1.5g

INGREDIENTS

2 tbsp plus 1 tsp olive oil

¼ cup shallots, sliced

2 sprigs fresh thyme

Himalayan pink salt

Ground black pepper

2 tbsp red wine vinegar

1 tbsp grass fed butter

1 ½ lbs skirt steak, cut into 4 pieces

10 oz cremini mushrooms, stems trimmed and thinly sliced

6 cups watercress, thick stems removed

Please See Next Page

INSTRUCTIONS

1. Season steak with salt and ground pepper. Set aside.

2. Heat oil in a large skillet over medium heat.

3. Sauté shallots, thyme, ¼ tsp salt and ¼ tsp ground pepper, stirring frequently until shallots are tender, about 4 to 6 minutes.

4. Remove skillet from heat. Discard thyme sprigs.

5. Add vinegar and butter to the sautéed mixture. Transfer in a small bowl and set aside.

6. Heat the same skillet over medium heat with 1 tsp of oil.

7. Cook steak for about 3 to 5 minutes per side (for medium-rare).

8. Transfer steak on a plate and let rest for 5 minutes.

9. Meanwhile, heat skillet with the remaining oil over medium heat.

10. Sauté mushrooms with ¼ tsp salt and ¼ tsp ground black pepper, stirring frequently for 4 to 6 minutes or until slightly golden.

11. Stir in watercress and cook for 2 to 4 minutes more.

12. Serve steak with sautéed watercress, top with the shallots.

13. Eat, Enjoy and Be Healthy!

Skillet-Roasted Strip Steaks
With Pebre Sauce & Avocados

SERVINGS: 4   COOK TIME: 30 MINUTES

Nutritional Facts

Calories	Protein	Fat	Carbs	Dietary Fiber	Sugar
560	45g	33g	20g	8.5g	8g

INGREDIENTS

Pebre Sauce

1/2 cup finely chopped sweet onion, such as Vidalia or Walla Walla

1 medium-large tomato, seeded and diced

1/3 cup chopped fresh cilantro

2 tablespoons minced jalapeño, or serrano pepper

2 tablespoons red-wine or cider vinegar

1 clove garlic, minced

1/4 teaspoon kosher salt

Steak

3/4 teaspoon paprika

3/4 teaspoon ground cumin

3/4 teaspoon dried oregano

3/4 teaspoon kosher salt, divided

1/2 teaspoon ground pepper

4 New York strip (about 1 pound)

top loin steaks, trimmed

2 teaspoons olive oil

2 avocados, pitted and peeled

Please See Next Page

INSTRUCTIONS

1. To prepare Pebre Sauce: Place onion in a medium bowl, cover with ice water and let soak for 10 to 20 minutes. Drain. Combine the onion, tomato, cilantro, jalapeño (or serrano), vinegar, garlic and 1/4 teaspoon salt in a medium bowl.

2. Preheat oven to 325°F.

3. To prepare steak: Mix paprika, cumin, oregano, 1/2 teaspoon salt and pepper in a small bowl. Rub the spice mixture evenly over both sides of steaks.

4. 4. just until browned, 1 to 2 minutes per side. Transfer the pan to the oven and roast the steaks 5 to 7 minutes for medium-rare, depending on thickness. Transfer to a clean cutting board. Tent with foil and let rest for 5 minutes.

5. Meanwhile, mash avocados with the remaining 1/4 teaspoon salt in a small bowl.

6. Carve the steak into thin slices. Serve with the avocado and Pebre Sauce.

Steak With
Mustard Crust

SERVINGS: 4 PREP TIME: 10 MINUTES COOK TIME: 15 MINUTES

Nutritional Facts

Calories	Protein	Fat	Carbs	Dietary Fiber	Sugar
370	50g	18g	1g	0g	0.5g

INGREDIENTS

2 cloves garlic, minced

3 tsp Dijon mustard

1 tbsp Worcestershire sauce

1 tsp ground dry mustard

¼ tsp Himalayan Pink salt

½ tsp ground black pepper

1 ½ lbs top grass fed round steak

INSTRUCTIONS

1. Preheat the oven broiler. Line a broiler pan with aluminum foil.

2. In a small bowl, combine garlic, Dijon mustard, Worcestershire sauce, mustard, salt and pepper. Whisk to combine.

3. Coat steak evenly with Dijon mustard. Set aside for 10 minutes.

4. Place steak on top of the foil and broil to desired doneness (4 minutes per side for medium rare).

5. Transfer steak to a cutting board and let rest for 10 minutes.

6. Cut steak into thin slices and serve immediately.

7. Eat, Enjoy and Be Healthy!

Steak With
Spicy Beans and Tomatoes

SERVINGS: 4 COOK TIME: 30 MINUTES

Nutritional Facts

Calories	Protein	Fat	Carbs	Dietary Fiber	Sugar
475	44g	24g	20g	9g	6g

INGREDIENTS

5 ½ tbsp olive oil

2 strip steak (grass fed), about 1 ½ lbs total

4 cups grape tomatoes

¼ cup fresh oregano leaves

1 ½ lbs green beans, trimmed

2 cloves garlic, thinly sliced

½ tsp crushed pepper flakes

Himalayan pink salt and
ground black pepper, to taste

INSTRUCTIONS

1. Boil water in a large saucepan. Season steak with salt and pepper.

2. Meanwhile, heat 2 tsp of oil in a skillet over medium heat.

3. Cook steak on both sides until you reached the desired doneness. 4 to 6 minutes per side for medium rare.

4. Transfer cooked steak to a plate and let rest for 5 minutes.

5. Wipe skillet, then add 1 tsp of oil and heat over medium heat. Add tomatoes and a dash of salt and pepper. Cook for about 6 minutes or until tomatoes soften.

6. Stir in oregano.

7. When the water is boiling, add green beans and cook just until tender, about 3 minutes. Drain.

8. Wipe out saucepan and heat 3 tbsp of oil over medium heat. Sauté garlic, until fragrant, about 2 minutes.

9. Add cooked green beans. Season with salt and ground black pepper. Toss to combine. Sprinkle red pepper flakes.

10. Serve cooked green beans with steak and tomatoes.

11. Eat, Enjoy and Be Healthy!

Beef Stew

SERVINGS: 6   PREP TIME: 10 MINUTES   COOK TIME: 20 MINUTES

Nutritional Facts

Calories	Protein	Fat	Carbs	Dietary Fiber	Sugar
390	41g	23g	5g	1g	1g

INGREDIENTS

2 lbs boneless beef sirloin steak, cut into 1-inch cubes

3 tbsp coconut flour

2 tbsp vegetable oil, divided

1 package McCormick® Beef Stew Seasoning Mix

3 cups water

5 cups frozen vegetables for stew

INSTRUCTIONS

1.   Dust beef with flour. Set aside.

2.   Heat a non-stick skillet or Dutch oven on medium-high heat.

3.   When oil is hot, add ½ of the beef and cook until brown on all sides.

4.   Repeat with remaining beef.

5.   Add the remaining 1 tbsp of oil. Return beef to skillet.

6.   Stir in Seasoning mix, water and vegetables. Bring to a boil.

7.   Eat, Enjoy and be Healthy!

Philly Cheesesteak
Stuffed Peppers

SERVINGS: 4   PREP TIME: 10 MINUTES   COOK TIME: 15 MINUTES

Nutritional Facts

Calories	Protein	Fat	Carbs	Dietary Fiber	Sugar
380	35g	19g	17g	7g	10g

INGREDIENTS

2 yellow onions, thinly sliced

8 oz mushrooms, sliced

1 lb ground beef

2 tbsp hot sauce

3 tbsp Worcestershire sauce

2 bell peppers

4 oz Provolone cheese (optional)

Butter (for greasing the pan)

INSTRUCTIONS

1. Preheat the oven to 350°F.

2. Cut each bell pepper in half, removed seeds and membranes. Place bell peppers on a roasting tin, cut side down and bake for about 15 minutes or until tender.

3. Meanwhile, melt butter in a large skillet over medium heat. Add onions and mushrooms and sauté until vegetables are golden. Transfer to a plate and set aside.

4. Heat the skillet and add ground beef, hot sauce, Worcestershire sauce and salt.

5. Sauté the mixture until beef is brown and the liquid has evaporated. Bring onions and mushrooms back to the skillet. Mix well to combine.

6. Stuffed roasted bell pepper with the ground beef mixture. Sprinkle cheese on top (optional).

7. Roast stuffed bell peppers until cheese melts.

8. Eat, Enjoy and Be Healthy!

Steak Tacos With
Mushroom and Pablanos

SERVINGS: 6 PREP TIME: 10 MINUTES COOK TIME: 15 MINUTES

Nutritional Facts

Calories	Protein	Fat	Carbs	Dietary Fiber	Sugar
385	36g	23g	8g	2g	1g

INGREDIENTS

Steak Marinade

¼ cup olive oil

4 cloves garlic, minced

3 tbsp lime juice

1 tsp ground cumin

1 tsp salt

½ tsp fresh ground black pepper

Garnish

Gluten free tortillas

Fresh cilantro, chopped

Avocado slices

Lime wedges

Salsa verde

Goat cheese, crumbled

Tacos

2 tbsp olive oil

1.5 lbs grass fed flank steak

2 large poblano peppers, cut into 2-inch strips

1 medium yellow onion, thinly sliced

8 oz baby Portobello mushrooms, sliced or quartered

3 cloves garlic, crushed

½ tsp Himalayan pink salt

¼ tsp ground cumin

¼ tsp ground black pepper

Please See Next Page

INSTRUCTIONS

1. In a large Ziploc bag, combine all ingredients for the marinade. Add flank steak and massage with the marinade completely. Seal and refrigerate for about 15 minutes or overnight for best flavor.

2. When ready to make tacos, thaw steak to room temperature.

3. Heat grill pan or skillet over medium-high heat. Add flank steak to the grill pan. Discard marinade.

4. Cook steak for about 4-5 minutes on each side until your desired doneness is achieved.

5. Transfer grilled steak on a plate and let rest for 10 minutes. Sliced into thin strips.

6. Meanwhile, heat oil in a sauté pan over medium-high heat. Sauté onions and poblano peppers for about 5 minutes until onions are soft and translucent.

7. Add mushrooms and sauté for 2 minutes more. Stir in garlic, salt, cumin and ground black pepper. Sauté until fragrant. Adjust seasonings according to your taste.

8. Transfer vegetable mixture on a platter and set aside.

9. Return sauté pan back to the heat to warm tortillas for about 10 seconds per side to soften. Remove from heat.

10. To assemble tacos, layer sliced steak into warm tortillas followed by veggies and chopped cilantro.

11. Serve with avocado slices, lime wedges and salsa verde.

12. Eat, Enjoy and Be Healthy!

Grilled Steak With
Poblano-Corn Sauce

SERVINGS: 2 COOK TIME: 30 MINUTES

Nutritional Facts

Calories	Protein	Fat	Carbs	Dietary Fiber	Sugar
720	30g	54g	28g	5g	9g

INGREDIENTS

2 ears of corn, husked

1 large poblano chile

¼ cup extra virgin olive oil, plus more for grilling

Salt, to taste

Freshly ground black pepper, to taste

1 ¾ lbs skirt steak, cut into 5-inch pieces

INSTRUCTIONS

1. Preheat the grill pan.
2. Rub corn and poblano chile with oil and grill over high heat until corn brown slightly and the poblano chile is completely charred but still firm, about 3 minutes.
3. Remove the skin off poblano, then diced or chopped roughly.
4. Separate kernels from the corn cob. Place half of poblano and half of corn kernels into a blender. Add 2 tbsp of olive oil and 2 tbsp of water. Blend to a chunky sauce.
5. Season to taste with salt and ground black pepper.
6. In a small bowl, combine remaining diced poblanos, corn kernels and 2 tbsp of oil. Season with a dash of salt and ground black pepper.
7. Rub steak generously with oil. Season with salt and ground black pepper.
8. Grill steak over high heat, turning occasionally until charred on both sides, about 6-7 minutes.
9. Transfer grilled steak on to a cutting board and let rest for 5 minutes, then slice thinly across the grain.
10. To serve, spoon corn-poblano sauce on a plate, top with slices of grilled steak.
11. Spoon salsa over the steak.
12. Eat, Enjoy and Be Healthy!

Grilled Beef Tenderloin With
Mustard & Herbs Crust

SERVINGS: 4   PREP TIME: 10 MINUTES   COOK TIME: 20 MINUTES

Nutritional Facts

Calories	Protein	Fat	Carbs	Dietary Fiber	Sugar
275	38.5g	12g	0.5g	0.5g	0g

INGREDIENTS

1 (1 ½ lbs) beef tenderloin, trimmed

Coconut oil spray

1 tsp Himalayan pink salt

1 tsp freshly ground black pepper

1/3 cup fresh parsley, finely chopped

2 tbsp fresh thyme, chopped

1 ½ tbsp fresh rosemary, finely chopped

3 tbsp Dijon mustard

INSTRUCTIONS

1. Prepare the grill. Lightly spray with cooking oil spray.

2. Lightly coat beef with cooking spray. Season with salt and pepper.

3. Grill beef for about 30 minutes or until desired degree of doneness has achieved. Let beef stand 10 minutes.

4. Lay an 1x15-inch sheet of plastic wrap on a working table. Sprinkle parsley, thyme, and rosemary in an even layer.

5. Brush beef with mustard evenly. Place beef in herb mixture on plastic wrap. Roll beef over herbs, pressing gently.

6. Slice beef thinly and serve.

7. Eat, Enjoy and Be Healthy!

Chicken and Avocado Soup

SERVINGS: 4   COOK TIME: 20 minutes

Nutritional Facts

Calories	Protein	Fat	Carbs	Dietary Fiber	Sugar
220	31g	9g	5.5g	4g	1g

INGREDIENTS

6 cups organic chicken broth

1 tsp Sriracha sauce

1 lb boneless, skinless chicken breast, diced

1 ripe avocado, pitted and diced

3 ½ stalks scallions

1 clove garlic, crushed

Himalayan pink salt and ground black pepper, to taste

INSTRUCTIONS

1. Cook chicken on George Foreman Grill for about 5 minutes or until the meat is white all the way through or bake if you prefer but the George Foreman is the faster option.

2. Using a heavy soup pot or pan, heat chicken broth over medium high heat. Stir in Sriracha sauce. Lower the heat and let the broth simmer.

3. Meanwhile, slice scallions. Separate white and green parts.

4. Add chicken and white part of scallions into the simmering broth, while stirring.

5. Stir in crushed garlic, then bring the soup back to simmering for another 10 minutes.

6. Add a dash of salt and pepper to taste.

7. To serve, ladle soup into individual bowls, top with diced avocados and sliced green scallions.

8. Eat, Enjoy and Be Healthy!

Buffalo Chicken Salad

SERVINGS: 4 COOK TIME: 15 minutes

Nutritional Facts

Calories	Protein	Fat	Carbs	Dietary Fiber	Sugar
210	30g	7g	6g	2g	4g

INGREDIENTS

4 pieces chicken breast, grilled or baked, diced

2 large red or yellow bell peppers, diced

3 tbsp hot sauce

2 tbsp Greek yogurt or mayo

1 tsp garlic powder

Himalayan pink salt, to taste

3 stalks green onions, chopped

½ cup celery, chopped

Garnishes

Blue cheese, crumbled

INSTRUCTIONS

1. Grill chicken until white all the way through and dice up.

2. In a large mixing bowl, combine all ingredients. Mix gently.

3. Transfer to a salad bowl and serve with a garnish of crumbled blue cheese on top.

4. Eat, Enjoy and Be Healthy!

Almond
Crusted Chicken
Fingers

SERVINGS: 4 PREP TIME: 11 minutes COOK TIME: 16-18 minutes

Nutritional Facts

Calories	Protein	Fat	Carbs	Dietary Fiber	Sugar
245	33g	11g	3g	2g	0.5g

INGREDIENTS

1 lb chicken tenders (or skinless chicken breast, cut into strips)

1 egg, beaten

½ cup almond meal

½ tsp Himalayan pink salt

¾ tsp paprika

½ tsp ground coriander seeds

½ tsp ground cumin seeds

INSTRUCTIONS

1. Preheat the oven to 425°F degrees. Line baking sheet with parchment paper. Set aside.

2. In a large bowl, combine almond meal, salt, paprika, coriander and cumin seeds. Mix well.

3. Place beaten eggs in a separate bowl.

4. Pat-dry chicken tender or strips using a kitchen towel.

5. Dip chicken in egg, then roll in the almond mixture. Make sure that the chicken is well coated with almonds.

6. Arrange in a prepared baking sheet and bake until completely cooked, about 16-18 minutes, turning once during cooking time.

7. Eat, Enjoy and Be Healthy!

Spicy Chicken Salad With
Mango and Avocado

SERVINGS: 1 COOK TIME: 5 minutes

Nutritional Facts

Calories	Protein	Fat	Carbs	Dietary Fiber	Sugar
697	40g	36g	52g	31g	21g

INGREDIENTS

1 head romaine lettuce

2 cups chicken, shredded

1/2 ripe mango, peeled and diced

1 ripe avocado, diced

½ tsp chili powder

½ tsp ground cumin

Himalayan pink salt and fresh ground black pepper, to taste

INSTRUCTIONS

1. Grill chicken until it is white all the way through. Then shred it as thin as possible.

2. In a large mixing bowl, place shredded lettuce.

3. In a separate bowl, place shredded chicken and a little water, just to moisten the chicken. Microwave on high for about 15 seconds. Stir in chili powder and ground cumin.

4. Toss chicken and shredded lettuce. Top with diced mango and avocado.

5. Serve immediately.

6. Eat, Enjoy and Be Healthy!

Thai
Chicken Salad

SERVINGS: 4 PREP TIME: 15 MINUTES

Nutritional Facts

Calories	Protein	Fat	Carbs	Dietary Fiber	Sugar
575	40g	27g	42.5g	10g	17g

INGREDIENTS

3 cups cooked chicken, shredded

2 cups purple cabbage, shredded

1 cup green cabbage, shredded

1 ripe avocado, diced

½ ripe mango, diced

1 large carrot, shredded

1 large red bell pepper, diced

1 cup fresh cilantro, roughly chopped

½ cup green onions, chopped

¼ cup cashew nuts, chopped

Cashew Dressing

½ cup organic cashew butter

3 tbsp hot water

2 tbsp rice wine vinegar

2 ½ tbsp coconut aminos

2 tbsp honey

¼ tsp sesame oil

Juice of 1 lime

Pinch of red pepper flakes

INSTRUCTIONS

1. Grill or broil chicken until it is cooked.

2. Shred chicken.

3. Combine Thai salad ingredients in a large bowl. Stir gently to combine.

4. In another bowl, combine dressing ingredients and mix well.

5. Add a teaspoon of hot water from time to time while stirring until you've reached your desired consistency.

6. Drizzle cashew dressing over salad just before serving.

7. Eat, Enjoy and Be Healthy!

Baked Chicken Tenders With
Hemp Seeds Crust

SERVINGS: 5 PREP TIME: 15 MINUTES COOK TIME: 15 MINUTES

Nutritional Facts

Calories	Protein	Fat	Carbs	Dietary Fiber	Sugar
375	33g	22g	11g	10g	1g

INGREDIENTS

5/8 cup hemp seeds

½ cup ground almonds or almond meal

1 tsp garlic powder

½ tsp paprika

½ tsp Himalayan pink salt

¼ tsp fresh ground black pepper

Pinch of cayenne pepper

1 ½ lbs boneless, skinless chicken breast, sliced into thick strips

2 large organic eggs, beaten

¼ teaspoon coconut oil cooking spray, as needed for greasing

INSTRUCTIONS

1. Preheat oven to 400°F degrees. Line baking sheet with parchment paper.

2. In a large mixing bowl, combine hemp seeds, garlic powder, ground almonds, paprika, salt, ground black pepper and cayenne pepper. Whisk to combine.

3. Dip chicken strips in beaten eggs, then dredge with hemp seeds mixture.

4. Place chicken strips into the prepared baking sheet and spray with cooking oil spray.

5. Bake chicken strips for about 15-20 minutes, turning once halfway during cooking time, until chicken strips are cooked and lightly golden.

6. Place baked chicken strips on a serving platter and served with your favorite dipping sauce.

7. Eat, Enjoy and Be Healthy!

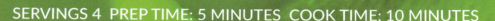

White
Chili Chicken

SERVINGS 4 PREP TIME: 5 MINUTES COOK TIME: 10 MINUTES

Nutritional Facts

Calories	Protein	Fat	Carbs	Dietary Fiber	Sugar
400	56g	5g	33g	9g	4g

INGREDIENTS

6 cups organic chicken broth

4 cups chicken, cooked and shredded

2 (15.50-oz) cans navy beans, drained

2 cups salsa verde

2 tsp ground cumin

Optional Toppings

Diced avocado

Freshly chopped cilantro

Shredded cheese

Chopped green onions

INSTRUCTIONS

1. Grill chicken until white all the way through and shred

2. In a medium saucepan, combine shredded chicken, chicken broth, navy beans, salsa verde and ground cumin. Stir to combine. Bring to a boil.

3. When boiling, reduce the heat, cover and let the mixture simmer for about 5 minutes.

4. Serve warm with your choice of toppings.

5. Eat, Enjoy and Be Healthy!

Chicken
Pesto Soup

SERVINGS: 4   PREP TIME: 3 MINUTES   COOK TIME: 12 MINUTES

Nutritional Facts

Calories	Protein	Fat	Carbs	Dietary Fiber	Sugar
440	47g	14g	30g	9g	3g

INGREDIENTS

4 cups chicken broth

3 cups fresh spinach

2 ½ cups chicken, cooked and shredded

2 (15.50 oz) cans navy beans, drained

1/3 cup pesto

2 tablespoons grated Parmesan cheese, for toppings

INSTRUCTIONS

1. Grill chicken until white all the way through and shred.

2. In a medium saucepan, combine shredded chicken, chicken stock, spinach and navy beans. Bring to a boil over high heat, then lower the heat and let the mixture simmer.

3. Stir in pesto. Simmer for another 2 minutes.

4. Serve warm, top with grated Parmesan cheese.

5. Eat, Enjoy and Be Healthy!

Grilled Buttermilk
Chicken Breast

SERVINGS 8

Nutritional Facts

Calories	Protein	Fat	Carbs	Dietary Fiber	Sugar
250	36g	10g	3g	0g	3g

INGREDIENTS

8 chicken fillets

1 cup buttermilk

1 tbsp Dijon mustard

1 tbsp raw honey

1 tbsp fresh rosemary, chopped

½ tsp dried thyme

½ tsp dried sage

½ tsp dried marjoram

½ tsp ground black pepper

INSTRUCTIONS

1. In a bowl, combine buttermilk, mustard, honey, rosemary, thyme, sage, marjoram, ground black pepper and salt. Mix well to combine.

2. Place chicken breast in a Ziploc bag and pour over the buttermilk mixture. Massage chicken with the marinade.

3. Marinate chicken for about 15 minutes, then grill over medium heat until cooked.

4. Eat, Enjoy and Be Healthy!

Sweet Potatoes
Stuff with BBQ Chicken

SERVINGS: 4 COOK TIME: 30 MINUTES

Nutritional Facts

Calories	Protein	Fat	Carbs	Dietary Fiber	Sugar
295	36g	4g	25g	2.5g	10.5g

INGREDIENTS

2 pieces medium sweet potatoes, halved

1 lb boneless, skinless chicken breast, cooked and shredded

1/3 cup barbecue sauce

Chopped parsley or chopped green onions (garnish)

INSTRUCTIONS

1. Preheat oven to 425°F.

2. Place sweet potatoes, cut side up on a baking sheet and roast for about 15 minutes or until tender. Roasting time depends on the size of sweet potatoes.

3. Meanwhile, in a saucepan, combine shredded chicken and chicken BBQ sauce and heat over medium high heat for about 5 minutes.

4. Divide the chicken mixture on each half of potatoes.

5. Serve garnish with chopped fresh parsley or green onions.

6. Eat, Enjoy and Be Healthy!

Chicken Breast With
Olives And Tomatoes

SERVINGS: 4   COOK TIME: 15 MINUTES

Nutritional Facts

Calories	Protein	Fat	Carbs	Dietary Fiber	Sugar
300	39g	15g	2g	0.5g	1.5g

INGREDIENTS

4 (6 oz) boneless, skinless chicken breast, halved

1 cup cherry or grape tomatoes, halved

3 tbsp oil and vinegar dressing, divided

20 olives, halved

½ cup feta cheese, crumbled

2 tbsp cream cheese or sour cream

½ small fennel bulb, thinly shaved with a peeler

INSTRUCTIONS

1. Preheat the grill to medium high heat. Coat the grill with cooking oil spray.

2. Season chicken with ¼ tsp salt and ¼ tsp ground black pepper. Grill chicken for 6 minutes per side or until completely cooked. Set aside and keep warm.

3. In a skillet, combine tomatoes, half of the dressing and olives. Cook over medium high heat for 2-3 minutes or until tomatoes are soft.

4. Brush the remaining half of the dressing to the grilled chicken. Cut each chicken breast into 3/4 –inch slices.

5. Top each breast with tomato mixture.

6. Serve with a sprinkle of grated cheese and torn fresh basil, if desired.

7. Eat, Enjoy and Be Healthy!

Chicken
Puttanesca
Pasta

SERVINGS: 4   COOK TIME: 15 -20 MINUTES

Nutritional Facts

Calories	Protein	Fat	Carbs	Dietary Fiber	Sugar
540	46g	15g	55g	4g	6g

INGREDIENTS

8 oz brown rice angel hair pasta, uncooked

2 tsp olive oil

4 (6 oz) boneless, skinless chicken breast, cut into 1-inch pieces

½ tsp Himalayan pink salt

2 cups tomato-basil pasta sauce

¼ cup Kalamata olives, pitted and coarsely chopped

1 tbsp capers

INSTRUCTIONS

1. Cook pasta according to package instructions, omitting the salt. Drain.

2. Heat the oil in a skillet over medium high heat. Add chicken. Season with salt. Cook chicken until brown, about 5 minutes.

3. Add in pasta sauce, olives, capers and crushed red pepper. Let the mixture simmer for about 5 minutes or until chicken is done.

4. To serve, divide cooked pasta on 4 serving plates, top with 1 ½ cup of chicken mixture.

5. Sprinkle each with 1 tbsp of grated cheddar cheese and a garnish of chopped basil leaves, if desired.

6. Eat, Enjoy and Be Healthy!

Chicken Shawarma

SERVINGS: 4   COOK TIME: 30 MINUTES

Nutritional Facts

Calories	Protein	Fat	Carbs	Dietary Fiber	Sugar
310	30g	11g	23g	1g	5.5g

INGREDIENTS

2 tbsp fresh lemon juice

1 tsp curry powder

2 tsp extra virgin olive oil

¾ tsp Himalayan pink salt

½ tsp ground cumin

3 garlic cloves, minced

1 lb skinless, boneless chicken breast, cut into 16 strips

Sauce

½ cup Greek-style yogurt

2 tbsp tahini

2 tsp fresh lemon juice

¼ tsp Himalayan pink salt

1 garlic clove, minced

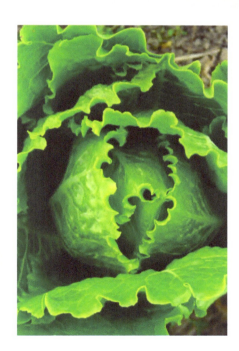

Other Ingredients

Coconut oil cooking spray

4 (6-inch each) pita bread (gluten free)

1 cup romaine lettuce, chopped

8 (1/4-inch thick) tomato slices

INSTRUCTIONS

1. Preheat the grill to medium high heat. Spray the grill with cooking oil spray.

2. Meanwhile, prepare the chicken first by combining all chicken ingredients in a large bowl. Let it stand at room temperature for 20-25 minutes.

3. In another bowl, combine all sauce ingredients and whisk until smooth.

4. Prepare 8 (12-inch) skewers and thread 2 strips of chicken into each skewers.

5. Grill chicken for about 5 minutes on each side or until done.

6. Grill pita bread for about 1 minute per side or until lightly toasted.

7. To serve, place 1 pita each of the 4 plates, top with ¼ cup each of lettuce and 2 slices of tomato.

8. Top each serving with 4 chicken pieces and drizzle each serving with 2 tbsp of sauce.

9. Eat, Enjoy and Be Healthy!

Chicken And Black Bean Chilaquiles

SERVINGS: 6   COOK TIME: 25 MINUTES

Nutritional Facts

Calories	Protein	Fat	Carbs	Dietary Fiber	Sugar
475	33g	11g	61g	17g	4g

INGREDIENTS

Coconut oil cooking spray

1 cup onion, thinly sliced

5 garlic cloves, minced

3 cups chicken breast, cooked and shredded

1 (15 oz) can black beans, rinsed and drained

1 cup fat free, less sodium chicken broth

1 (7 ¾-oz) can salsa

15 (6-ich) tortillas (gluten free), cut into 1-inch strips

1 cup (4 oz) queso blanco, shredded

INSTRUCTIONS

1. Preheat the oven to 450°F.
2. Heat a large skillet over medium high heat and spray with cooking oil spray.
3. Sauté onion for about 5 minutes or until soft and golden brown. Add garlic and sauté for 1 minute. Add chicken and sauté for a few seconds.
4. Transfer cooked chicken mixture into a large bowl and stir in beans.
5. Using the same skillet, add broth and salsa. Bring to a boil. Reduce the heat and let the mixture simmer for 5 minutes. Turn off the heat and set aside.
6. Arrange half of tortilla strips in a baking sheet coated with cooking oil spray.
7. Layer half of chicken mixture over tortillas, top with remaining tortillas and chicken mixture.
8. Pour broth mixture evenly over the chicken mixture. Sprinkle with grated cheese on top.
9. Bake until tortillas are lightly brown and the cheese melts, about 10-12 minutes.
10. Eat, Enjoy and Be Healthy!

Chicken Creole

SERVINGS: 4 (1 ½ cup per serving)

Nutritional Facts

Calories	Protein	Fat	Carbs	Dietary Fiber	Sugar
380	35g	3g	52g	4g	17g

INGREDIENTS

4 pieces boneless chicken breast, cut into ¾-inch strips

2 cups tomatoes, chopped

1 cup chili sauce

1 ½ cups green bell pepper, chopped

½ cup celery, chopped

½ cup onion, chopped2 cloves garlic, minced

1 tbsp fresh basil

1 tbsp fresh parsley

¼ tsp red pepper flakes

¼ tsp Himalayan pink salt

Cooking oil spray

2 cups of brown rice (cooked)

INSTRUCTIONS

1. Spray skillet with cooking oil spray and preheat skillet over medium high heat.

2. Add "boil in bag" of brown rice to boiling water and cook for 10 minutes, remove and set aside.

3. Stir-fry chicken until no longer pink, about 3-5 minutes. Reduce the heat to low.

4. Stir in tomatoes, chili sauce, bell pepper, celery, onion, basil, parsley, red pepper flakes and salt. Bring to a boil.

5. Lower the heat, cover the skillet and let the mixture simmer for 10 minutes.

6. Serve over brown rice.

7. Eat, Enjoy and Be Healthy!

Chicken Scallopine
Over Broccoli
Rabe

SERVINGS: 4   COOK TIME: 10-15 MINUTES

Nutritional Facts

Calories	Protein	Fat	Carbs	Dietary Fiber	Sugar
310	33g	8g	27g	4.5g	13.5g

INGREDIENTS

1 tbsp olive oil

1/3 cup Italian bread crumbs (gluten free)

¼ tsp ground black pepper

1 lb chicken breast

½ cup dry white wine

½ cup less sodium chicken broth (fat free)

3 tbsp fresh lemon juice

1 tsp butter (grass fed)

1 lb broccoli rabe, cut into 3-inch pieces

2 tbsp fresh parsley, chopped

2 tbsp capers, rinsed and drain

4 lemon slices (optional)

INSTRUCTIONS

1. Heat the oil in a large non-stick skillet over medium high heat.

2. Meanwhile, combine bread crumbs and ground black pepper and place in a shallow dish. Dredge chicken with the bread crumbs mixture.

3. Cook chicken in hot oil, about 3 minutes per side or until done. Transfer cooked chicken on a plate and keep warm.

4. To the skillet, add wine, broth, juice and butter. Scrape sides and bottom of the skillet to loosen up browned bits.

5. Add in broccoli rabe. Cook broccoli until tender. Stir in chopped fresh parsley and capers.

6. Arrange broccoli rabe on a serving plate, top with chicken.

7. Garnish with lemon slices, if desired.

8. Eat, Enjoy and Be Healthy!

Herbed
Chicken Breast

SERVINGS: 4   COOK TIME: 30 MINUTES

Nutritional Facts

Calories	Protein	Fat	Carbs	Dietary Fiber	Sugar
380	41g	18g	13g	2g	4g

INGREDIENTS

Salsa

8 cups of water

½ lb tomatillos, husks and stems removed

1 garlic clove

1 Serrano chili

½ cup fresh cilantro, chopped

¼ cup onion, coarsely chopped

1 tsp fresh lime juice

¼ tsp Himalayan pink salt

Chicken

3 slices of white bread (gluten-free)

1 ½ lb skinless, boneless chicken breast, halved

½ tsp Himalayan pink salt

½ tsp ground cumin

¼ tsp ground red pepper

1 large egg, lightly beaten

1 tbsp olive oil

½ cup queso fresco, crumbled

Cilantro sprigs

Lime wedges

Please See Next Page

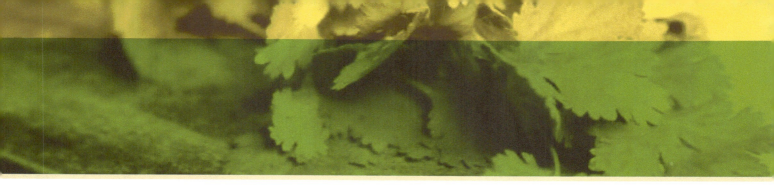

INSTRUCTIONS

1. Preheat the oven to 350°F.

2. First, prepare salsa by bringing water to a full boil. Add tomatillos, garlic and Serrano chili and boil for 7 minutes. Drain and rinsed with cold water.

3. In a bowl of a blender or food processor, combine tomatillos, garlic, chile, chopped cilantro, onion, lime juice and ¼ tsp of salt.

4. Pulse the mixture until coarsely chopped. Set aside.

5. To prepare the chicken, process the bread slices into a fine crumbs. You have to measure 1 ½ cups of bread crumbs.

6. Place bread crumbs evenly on the bottom of a baking sheet and bake until brown slightly. Let it cool.

7. Place chicken breast between sheets of heavy duty plastic wrap, then pound with a mallet or rolling pin into ½-inch thick.

8. Meanwhile, in a small bowl, combine ½ tsp salt, cumin and red pepper. Mix well. Rub this mixture evenly over chicken.

9. Place bread crumbs and beaten eggs in separate dish. Dip chicken in eggs, then coat with bread crumbs.

10. Heat the oil in a large skillet over medium high heat. Add chicken and fry for about 4 minutes on each side.

11. Arrange chicken on a serving plate, top with salsa. Sprinkle on top with grated cheese.

12. Serve garnish with fresh cilantro sprigs and lemon wedges, if desired.

13. Eat, Enjoy and Be Healthy!

Chicken Sautee

SERVINGS: 4   COOK TIME: 10-15 MINUTES

Nutritional Facts

Calories	Protein	Fat	Carbs	Dietary Fiber	Sugar
250	31g	7g	14g	1g	6g

INGREDIENTS

2 cups of brown rice

1 ½ lbs chicken breast tenders

1 tbsp cornstarch

1 tbsp fish sauce

4 tsp olive oil

1 cup onion, thinly sliced

2 tsp garlic, minced

1 tsp ground fresh ginger

½ cup light coconut milk

2 tbsp Sriracha sauce

1 tbsp cane sugar

1 tbsp fresh lime juice

2 tbsp fresh cilantro, chopped

4 lime wedges

INSTRUCTIONS

1. Cook rice according to package instructions.

2. In a bowl, combine chicken and fish sauce. Toss to combine.

3. Heat 1 tbsp of oil in a large skillet over medium high heat. Add chicken and sauté for 4-6 minutes or until cooked. Transfer to a platter and set aside.

4. Using the same skillet, heat remaining oil. Sauté onion, garlic and ginger for about 1 minute or until fragrant.

5. Add chicken back to the pan and sauté for another minute.

6. Stir in Sriracha sauce, sugar and fresh lime juice. Continue to cook until mixture is just heated through, stirring often.

7. Serve sautéed chicken over rice, lime wedges and a sprinkling of fresh cilantro.

8. Eat, Enjoy and Be Healthy!

Parmesan Crusted Chicken

SERVINGS: 4   COOK TIME: 15 MINUTES

Nutritional Facts

Calories	Protein	Fat	Carbs	Dietary Fiber	Sugar
235	31g	6g	14g	4.5g	2g

INGREDIENTS

Cooking oil spray

1/3 cup coconut flour

Himalayan pink salt

Freshly ground black pepper, to taste

1 lb boneless, skinless chicken breast, cut into ½-inch strips

1/3 cup milk

1/3 cup Parmesan cheese, grated

½ cup quick-cooking oats

¾ tsp garlic powder

¾ tsp onion powder

½ tsp dried oregano

INSTRUCTIONS

1. Preheat the oven to 400°F. Lightly spray a large baking sheet with cooking oil spray. Set aside.

2. Combine flour, ½ tsp salt and ½ tsp ground black pepper. Mix well and place in a shallow plate.

3. Place milk in a separate plate.

4. In a third separate plate, combine oats, grated Parmesan, garlic powder, onion powder and oregano. Mix well.

5. Dip chicken in flour, dip in milk, then roll in oatmeal mixture.

6. Arrange chicken evenly on a prepared baking sheet and bake for about 15 minutes or until chicken is golden brown and completely cooked.

7. Eat, Enjoy and Be Healthy!

Parmesan Chicken Cutlets

SERVINGS :4 (5 cutlets per serving)   COOK TIME: 5 MINUTES

Nutritional Facts

Calories	Protein	Fat	Carbs	Dietary Fiber	Sugar
430	33g	25g	18g	1g	1.5g

INGREDIENTS

1 lb boneless chicken breast, thinly sliced to about 20 pieces

¼ cup olive oil

2 large eggs, beaten

¾ cup Parmesan cheese, grated

¾ cup gluten free bread crumbs, Italian-style

INSTRUCTIONS

1. Dip chicken cutlets in eggs, then dredge with grated Parmesan cheese and roll in bread crumbs.

2. Heat olive oil in a skillet over medium high heat and pan-fry chicken cutlets until golden brown.

3. Eat, Enjoy and Be Healthy!

Palak Chicken

SERVINGS: 4   COOK TIME: 15-20 MINUTES

Nutritional Facts

Calories	Protein	Fat	Carbs	Dietary Fiber	Sugar
250	43g	2.5g	13g	3g	5g

INGREDIENTS

1 bunch of fresh spinach, shredded

1 ½ lbs chicken breast

Olive Oil

8 whole black peppercorns

2 bay leaves

8 cloves

5 green cardamom

2 onions, chopped

4 green chilies, chopped

8 garlic, chopped

1-inch piece ginger, grated

1 tbsp cumin

1 tbsp coriander powder

1 tbsp chili powder

1 tsp turmeric powder

1 tsp garam masala

5 tbsp yoghurt

Himalayan Pink Salt, to taste

INSTRUCTIONS

1. Heat the oil in a large sauté pan over medium high heat. Sauté peppercorns, bay leaves, cloves and cardamom for 1 minute.

2. Add onions, green chilies, ginger and garlic. Sauté until onions are soft.

3. Add chicken, cumin, coriander, turmeric, red chili powder and salt to taste. Stir-fry for a few minutes.

4. Add yogurt, 1 tbsp at a time until all yogurt has been use and chicken is lightly golden.

5. Add shredded spinach. Season with more salt if necessary. Cook until spinach is wilted and chicken is tender.

6. Add garam masala powder and continue to cook until gravy thickens.

7. Serve hot.

8. Eat, Enjoy and Be Healthy!

Orange Chicken

SERVINGS: 6   PREP TIME: 10 MINUTES   COOK TIME: 10 MINUTES

Nutritional Facts

Calories	Protein	Fat	Carbs	Dietary Fiber	Sugar
300	33g	13g	12g	0g	11g

INGREDIENTS

Chicken

2 lbs boneless, skinless chicken breasts, cut into bite-sized pieces

Himalayan pink salt

Ground pepper, to taste

2 tbsp olive oil

½ cup orange chicken sauce

2 bay leaves

Orange Sauce

3 cloves garlic, minced

½ cup orange juice

½ cup honey

1/3 cup coconut aminos

¼ cup rice wine vinegar

3 tbsp cornstarch

½ tsp ground ginger

½ tsp ground white pepper

Zest of 1 orange

Red pepper flakes

Quinoa

1 cup dry quinoa

2 cups chicken broth

Toppings

Sliced green onions

Toasted sesame seeds

Orange zest

Please See Next Page

INSTRUCTIONS

1. Cook quinoa in chicken broth until done. Set aside and keep warm.

2. Prepare the chicken, season with salt and pepper.

3. Heat oil in a sauté pan or skillet over medium high heat. Sauté chicken for 4-6 minutes or until chicken browns slightly and is almost done.

4. In a bowl, combine all ingredients for the sauce. Mix well. Add 2-3 tbsp of honey for an added sweetness. Pour this to the chicken sauté and bring to a boil until thickened.

5. Serve orange chicken over cooked quinoa or hot cooked rice.

6. Garnish with sliced green onions, toasted sesame seeds and orange zest.

7. Eat, Enjoy and Be Healthy!

Teriyaki Chicken

SERVINGS: 4   PREP TIME: 10 MINUTES   COOK TIME: 20 MINUTES

Nutritional Facts

Calories	Protein	Fat	Carbs	Dietary Fiber	Sugar
325	37.5g	10.5g	21g	0.5g	19g

INGREDIENTS

1 (8 oz) can crushed pineapple

3 tbsp coconut aminos

2 tbsp honey or agave nectar

1 tsp fresh ginger, grated

1 clove garlic, minced

4 boneless (about 16 oz),

Skinless chicken breast

INSTRUCTIONS

1. First make the teriyaki sauce by combining crushed pineapple, honey, coconut aminos, garlic and ginger in a large bowl. Whisk to combine.

2. Divide the sauce. Pour half of the sauce in a Ziploc bag and reserve the other half.

3. Place chicken inside Ziploc bag with the marinade. Massage chicken with the marinade. Refrigerate for 10 minutes or overnight.

4. To cook the chicken, preheat the broiler and place the rack in the middle.

5. Place marinated chicken on a baking sheet lined with foil.

6. Spoon chunky pineapple/ginger from the marinade and scatter on top of chicken. Discard the liquid marinade.

7. Broil chicken for about 8-10 minutes per side or until completely cooked.

8. Meanwhile, in a small saucepan, heat the remaining marinade and simmer over low heat for 3 minutes or until slightly thickens.

9. Slice cooked chicken, arrange on a platter and drizzle teriyaki sauce over the top.

10. Eat, Enjoy and Be Healthy!

Lemon Chicken with
Asparagus

SERVINGS: 3   COOK TIME: 20 MINUTES

Nutritional Facts

Calories	Protein	Fat	Carbs	Dietary Fiber	Sugar
530	37g	28g	32g	6g	15g

INGREDIENTS

1 lbs boneless, skinless chicken breast

¼ cup coconut flour

½ tsp Himalayan pink salt

Ground black pepper, to taste

2 tbsp butter

1 tsp lemon pepper seasoning

2 cups asparagus, chopped

2 lemons, thinly sliced

2 tbsp butter

Fresh parsley (for garnish)

INSTRUCTIONS

1. Place chicken breast between sheets of heavy duty plastic wrap. Pound chicken with a mallet to about ¾-inch thick.
2. Place flour in a shallow dish. Season with salt and pepper.
3. Toss chicken with flour evenly.
4. Meanwhile, melt the butter in a skillet over medium high heat.
5. Sauté chicken breast for about 3-5 minutes on each side or until golden brown. While sautéing, sprinkle chicken with lemon pepper. Transfer cooked chicken on a plate.
6. Using the same pan, sauté chopped asparagus until bright green but still crisp. Transfer to a plate and set aside.
7. Arrange lemon slices on the bottom of pan and cook over low heat without stirring until it caramelize.
8. Add a tiny pat of butter to the pan so that the lemons wouldn't stick to the bottom. Remove lemon slices from pan, set aside.
9. To assemble, place cooked asparagus back to the pan, then place chicken on top of asparagus.
10. Place lemon slices on top.
11. Eat, Enjoy and Be Healthy!

Sesame Chicken with Broccoli

SERVINGS: 4   COOK TIME: 15 MINUTES

Nutritional Facts

Calories	Protein	Fat	Carbs	Dietary Fiber	Sugar
415	41g	17.5g	22.5g	3g	15g

INGREDIENTS

2 cups broccoli florets

1 large egg white

2 tbsp cornstarch

½ tsp salt

1 ½ lbs boneless, skinless chicken breast, cut into small chunks

1 tbsp vegetable or coconut oil

1 red bell pepper, seeded and diced

2 scallions, white and green parts separated, thinly sliced

1 garlic clove, minced

3 tbsp coconut aminos

1 tsp sesame oil

3 tbsp honey

2 tbsp sesame seeds

INSTRUCTIONS

1. Bring a pan of water to a boil and add broccoli florets. Lower the heat to a gentle simmer and cook until broccoli florets are crisp tender, about 2 minutes. Drain broccoli.

2. Meanwhile in a large bowl, combine egg white, cornstarch and salt. Whisk to combine. Add chicken and toss to combine.

3. Heat oil in a skillet over medium high heat. Fry chicken until done. Transfer to a bowl and keep warm.

4. Use the same skillet and oil to stir-fry bell peppers and white part of scallions, about 2 minutes. Stir in garlic and sauté for about 1 minute.

5. Stir in cooked chicken, tamari, sesame oil, sesame seeds and honey. Simmer until sauce has reduces and thickens, about 3 minutes.

6. Stir in broccoli florets and green scallions.

7. Serve over hot cooked brown or white rice.

8. Eat, Enjoy and Be Healthy!

Chicken Sauté With
Sage Butter

SERVINGS: 6   COOK TIME: 25 MINUTES

Nutritional Facts

Calories	Protein	Fat	Carbs	Dietary Fiber	Sugar
385	33g	17g	27.5g	22.5g	0.5g

INGREDIENTS

4 (6 oz each) boneless, skinless chicken breast, halved

¼ tsp salt

¼ tsp ground black pepper

Cooking oil spray

½ cup coconut flour

3 tbsp grass fed butter

2 sprigs fresh sage

1 tbsp shallots, minced

1 tsp fresh thyme, chopped

2 tbsp lemon juice

Fresh sage leaves (optional)

INSTRUCTIONS

1. Place each breast between sheets of heavy duty plastic wrap and pound with a mallet to about ¼-inch thick. Dredge chicken with flour.

2. Heat a large skillet over medium high heat and spray with cooking oil spray.

3. Sauté chicken for about 4 minutes on each side until done. Transfer to a plate and keep warm.

4. Melt butter using the same skillet. Add sprigs of fresh sage and cook with the butter until butter browns. Discard sage.

5. Add shallots and thyme to the browned butter and cook for about 30 seconds. Add lemon juice and cook for a few more seconds.

6. Serve chicken with a drizzle of browned sage butter, and a garnish of sage leaves.

7. Eat, Enjoy and Be Healthy!

Chicken
Cacciatore

SERVINGS: 4   PREP TIME: 12 MINUTES   COOK TIME: 20 MINUTES

Nutritional Facts

Calories	Protein	Fat	Carbs	Dietary Fiber	Sugar
400	40g	17g	12g	3g	5.5g

INGREDIENTS

2 tsp olive oil

4 boneless, skinless chicken breast, halved (about 24 oz.)

¾ tsp salt, divided

¼ tsp freshly ground black pepper

1 small yellow or green bell pepper, cut into thin strips

2 cups crimini mushrooms, sliced

½ cup dry red wine

1 ½ cups tomato and basil pasta sauce

2 tbsp fresh parsley, chopped

INSTRUCTIONS

1. Heat oil in a large skillet over medium high heat. Sauté chicken. Sprinkle with salt and ground black pepper.

2. Cook chicken for about 4 minutes per side. When done, transfer to a plate and set aside.

3. Use the same skillet to sauté the mushrooms and bell pepper. Season with salt. Saute for about 4 minutes, stirring frequently until mushrooms are soft.

4. Add wine and cook for 2 minutes. Stir in pasta sauce and cooked just until heated through.

5. Return chicken back to the skillet, lower the heat and let the mixture simmer for about 4 minutes.

6. Serve chicken with a garnish of fresh parsley.

7. Eat, Enjoy and Be Healthy!

Chicken and
Arugula Salad

SERVINGS: 1 COOK TIME: 15 MINUTES

Nutritional Facts

Calories	Protein	Fat	Carbs	Dietary Fiber	Sugar
380	33g	24.5g	6.5g	2.5g	3.5g

INGREDIENTS

1 tbsp olive oil

10 baby carrots, chopped

½ cup red cabbage, chopped

1 cup arugula

250g chicken, cut into cubes

2 tsp sunflower seeds

INSTRUCTIONS

1. Heat oil in a large skillet over medium high heat. Pan-fry cubed chicken, then transfer to a plate and set aside.

2. In a large salad bowl, combine arugula, carrots and cabbage. Toss to combine.

3. Transfer salad to a serving platter, top with sunflower seeds and cooked chicken.

4. Serve with your favorite dressing.

5. Eat, Enjoy and Be Healthy!

White Bean
Chicken Salad

SERVINGS: 4   COOK TIME: 25 MINUTES

Nutritional Facts

Calories	Protein	Fat	Carbs	Dietary Fiber	Sugar
525	40g	29g	25.5g	8g	4g

INGREDIENTS

1 clove garlic, peeled and smashed

¼ tsp salt

5 tbsp extra virgin olive oil

6 tbsp orange juice + more to taste

¼ cup white wine vinegar or red wine vinegar

1 tbsp Dijon mustard

SALAD

1 (15 oz) can cannellini beans, rinsed and drained

3 cups chicken breast, cooked and diced

2 cups zucchini or summer squash, diced

1 ½ cups celery, diced

¼ cup ricotta, halloumi or feta cheese, finely diced

1/3 cup oil-packed sundried tomatoes, chopped

1 cup fresh basil, coarsely chopped

2 cups escarole or romaine lettuce, torn

2 cups radicchio leaves, torn

Whole basil leaves (for garnish)

Please See Next Page

INSTRUCTIONS

1. To prepare the vinaigrette, in a small bowl, mash garlic with 1 tsp of salt until the texture is like a coarse paste.

2. Whisk in 5 tbsp of oil, 6 tbsp orange juice, vinegar and mustard, until well blended.

3. Add more orange juice a tbsp at a time until you reached your desired taste. Season with salt if desired. Set aside.

4. To prepare the salad, in a large bowl, combine chicken, beans, zucchini, celery, cheese and sundried tomatoes. Blend well.

5. Add chopped basil and ¾ cup of vinaigrette. Season with salt and pepper.

6. In a medium bowl, place escarole or romaine lettuce and radicchio. Toss in remaining vinaigrette.

7. Serve salad with a garnish of fresh basil leaves.

8. Eat, Enjoy and Be Healthy!

Greek-Style
Salad With Chicken

SERVINGS: 4   COOK TIME: 25 MINUTES

Nutritional Facts

Calories	Protein	Fat	Carbs	Dietary Fiber	Sugar
315	31g	16g	11g	3g	5.5g

INGREDIENTS

1/3 cup red wine vinegar

2 tbsp extra virgin olive oil

1 tbsp fresh dill or oregano, chopped

1 tsp garlic powder

¼ tsp Himalayan pink salt

¼ tsp fresh ground black pepper

6 cups romaine lettuce, chopped

16 oz chicken

2 tomatoes chopped

1 medium cucumber, peeled, seeded and chopped

½ cup red onion, finely chopped

½ cup ripe black olives, sliced

½ cup feta cheese, crumbled

INSTRUCTIONS

1. Grill chicken for 3-5 minutes each side or until done.
2. In a large bowl, whisk vinegar together with oil, dill or oregano, garlic powder, salt and pepper.
3. In a separate large bowl, combine lettuce, chicken, tomatoes, cucumber, onion, olives and feta cheese. Toss to combine.
4. Add dressing to the mixed salad vegetables and serve immediately.
5. Eat, Enjoy and Be Healthy!

Chicken With Sage And Dried Plums

SERVINGS: 4   COOK TIME: 20 MINUTES

Nutritional Facts

Calories	Protein	Fat	Carbs	Dietary Fiber	Sugar
380	32g	15g	28.5g	6.5g	11g

INGREDIENTS

4 (6 oz) skinless, boneless chicken breast

2 tbsp fresh sage, chopped

½ tsp Himalayan pink salt

¼ tsp ground black pepper

4 tsp olive oil

2 cups onion, thinly sliced

½ cup dry white wine

½ cup less sodium chicken broth (fat free)

12 pitted dried plums, halved

4 oz chopped cashews

1 ½ tsp balsamic vinegar

INSTRUCTIONS

1. Place chicken breast between each sheet of heavy duty plastic wrap and pound with a mallet to about 1/2-inch thick.

2. Season chicken with 1 tbsp of fresh sage, salt and 1/8 tsp ground black pepper.

3. Heat 2 tsp of oil in a large non-stick skillet over medium high heat. Pan-fry chicken for about 4 minutes on each side or until done. Transfer chicken to a plate and keep warm.

4. Use the same skillet to heat up 2 tsp of oil. Sauté onion until soft.

5. Stir in wine and broth and bring mixture to a boil.

6. Add remaining sage and dried plums. Continue to cook until mixture thickens.

7. Stir in 1/8 tsp of ground black pepper and vinegar.

8. Serve, top with chopped cashews.

9. Eat, Enjoy and Be Healthy!

Chicken Soup
Mexican-Style

SERVINGS: 4 (2 ½ cups per serving)
PREP TIME: 2   COOK TIME: 25 MINUTES

Nutritional Facts

Calories	Protein	Fat	Carbs	Dietary Fiber	Sugar
350	41.5g	15g	12g	0.5g	6g

INGREDIENTS

1 tbsp olive oil

1 small onion, chopped

1 jalapeno, diced (optional)

2 cloves garlic, minced

5 cups chicken broth (low sodium)

1 ½ lbs boneless, skinless chicken breast, cut into strips

2 cups of mild salsa

INSTRUCTIONS

1. In a large saucepan, heat oil over medium high heat. Sauté onion and jalapeno until soft, about 5 minutes. Stir in garlic and sauté for half minute.

2. Pour in broth and bring to a boil. Lower the heat, add chicken strips, then simmer the mixture until chicken is cooked, about 3 minutes.

3. Pour in salsa, Season with a dash of salt and ground black pepper. Continue to simmer the mixture until just heated through.

4. Serve hot.

5. Eat, Enjoy and Be Healthy!

Chicken Teriyaki

SERVINGS: 4   PREP TIME: 15   COOK TIME: 15 MINUTES

Nutritional Facts

Calories	Protein	Fat	Carbs	Dietary Fiber	Sugar
315	38g	10.5g	16.5g	0g	15.5g

INGREDIENTS

1 ½ cups pineapple juice

½ cup coconut aminos

1 tsp ground ginger

½ tsp garlic powder

¼ tsp ground pepper

4 boneless, skinless chicken breast (1 ½ pounds)

INSTRUCTIONS

1. In a large bowl, combine pineapple juice, coconut aminos, ground ginger, garlic powder and ground pepper. Mix well.

2. Marinate chicken breast in pineapple juice mixture. Refrigerate overnight.

3. Grill chicken breast on both sides until done.

4. Eat, Enjoy and Be Healthy!

Chicken Tangine
With Olives

SERVINGS: 4   COOK TIME: 25 MINUTES

Nutritional Facts

Calories	Protein	Fat	Carbs	Dietary Fiber	Sugar
450	35g	15g	43g	9.5g	13g

INGREDIENTS

1 tbsp olive oil

1 cup onion, chopped

1 tbsp ginger, minced

1 tsp ground cumin

¼ tsp ground cinnamon

1 (14 oz) can diced tomatoes

½ cup chicken broth (low-sodium)

1 cup frozen peas, thawed

¼ cup pitted Kalamata olives, coarsely chopped

1/3 cup raisins

16oz chicken

1 (15 oz) can chickpeas, drained and rinsed

INSTRUCTIONS

1. Grill and dice chicken.
2. Heat the oil in a large non-stick skillet over medium high heat.
3. Sauté onion, ginger, cumin and cinnamon. Cook for about 4-5 minutes, stirring frequently, then add tomatoes, chicken broth, frozen peas, olives and raisins.
4. Lower the heat and let the mixture simmer for about 7-8 minutes.
5. Add chicken and chickpeas and cook for 4 minutes.
6. Serve warm.
7. Eat, Enjoy and Be Healthy!

Chicken Curry
Thai-Style

SERVINGS: 4   COOK TIME: 15-20 MINUTES

Nutritional Facts

Calories	Protein	Fat	Carbs	Dietary Fiber	Sugar
595	40g	37g	25g	12g	3g

INGREDIENTS

1 cup shallots, thinly sliced

2 tbsp olive or grape seed oil

2 Serrano chilies, thinly sliced

1-inch piece of fresh ginger, sliced into thin strips

1 clove garlic, chopped

1 tsp ground turmeric

1 ½ cups of cabbage, sliced into ½-inch strips

1 carrot, peeled and thinly sliced

1 cup mushroom caps, sliced

14 oz light coconut milk

1 lb boneless, skinless chicken breast, cut into 1-inch chunks

2 tbsp coconut aminos

2 medium tomatoes, sliced into wedges

1 cup snow peas, halved

½ cup fresh basil leaves, torn into pieces

1 stalk scallion

1 cup jasmine rice, cooked

1 lime, cut into wedges

Please See Next Page

INSTRUCTIONS

1. Separate green and white part of scallion. Slice the green part into 1-inch length. Chop the white part.

2. Heat oil in a large sauté pan over medium high heat. Add shallots. Sauté for 2 minutes.

3. Add chilies, ginger, garlic and turmeric and sauté for another minute.

4. Add cabbage, carrots and mushrooms. Sauté for 2 minutes.

5. Pour in coconut milk and 1 cup of water. Bring mixture to a full boil.

6. Add chicken and coconut aminos, lower the heat and let the mixture simmer without a cover for about 5 minutes. Stir in tomatoes and snow peas. Cook and continue to simmer for 3 minutes.

7. Lastly, add basil and scallions. Simmer for 1 minute more.

8. Serve chicken curry over plain jasmine rice and lemon wedges.

9. Eat, Enjoy and Be Healthy!

Chicken With Chunky Vegetable Sauce

SERVINGS: 4   COOK TIME: 30 MINUTES

Nutritional Facts

Calories	Protein	Fat	Carbs	Dietary Fiber	Sugar
380	42g	15.5g	18g	3g	4g

INGREDIENTS

1 tbsp coconut flour

4 skinless, boneless chicken breast, halved (1 ½ pounds)

1 cup onion, finely chopped

1 tbsp olive oil

2 cloves garlic, minced

1 (14 ½-oz can) diced tomatoes

1 (14 oz can) artichoke hearts, drained and halved

1/3 cup chicken broth (low-sodium)

Ground black pepper

2 tsp capers drained or 2 tbsp pitted ripe olives, chopped

1 tbsp fresh oregano, snipped or 1 tsp dried oregano, crushed

2 cups cot cooked rice

Pitted ripe olives

Please See Next Page

INSTRUCTIONS

1. Coat chicken with flour, shaking off excess. Set aside.
2. Heat oil in a large skillet over medium high heat. Add shallots and sauté for about 3 minutes or until soft.
3. Stir in garlic and sauté for another minute. Push sauté mixture towards the edge of the skillet. Add chicken.
4. Brown chicken on both sides, then add tomatoes, artichokes and chicken broth. Sprinkle with a dash of ground black pepper. Stir occasionally. Bring to a boil.
5. Reduce heat, cover the skillet and let the mixture simmer until chicken is tender, about 10 minutes.
6. Scoop out chicken from the mixture, transfer to a platter and set aside.
7. Continue to simmer the tomato mixture, without cover for about 3 minutes or until you reached your desired consistency.
8. Stir in capers and oregano.
9. Serve chicken over rice, top with chunky vegetable sauce.
10. Garnish with fresh pitted olives, if desired.
11. Eat, Enjoy and Be Healthy!

Barbecue
Chicken Salad

SERVINGS: 4   COOK TIME: 15 MINUTES

Nutritional Facts

Calories	Protein	Fat	Carbs	Dietary Fiber	Sugar
410	35g	22g	17g	2.5g	10g

INGREDIENTS

Salad

4 boneless, skinless chicken breasts, halved (1 pound)

1 tsp olive oil

Himalayan pink salt and ground black pepper, to taste

4 tbsp barbecue sauce

10 cups romaine lettuce, finely shredded

2 cups tomatoes, seeded and chopped

1 ½ cup cucumber, seeded and diced

2 cups zucchini, diced

4 oz light cheddar cheese, shredded

½ cup red onion, chopped

Vinaigrette

¼ cup balsamic vinegar

2 tbsp Dijon mustard

1 tbsp honey

2 tbsp extra virgin olive oil

2 tbsp fresh basil leaves, finely chopped

Himalayan pink salt and ground black pepper to taste

Please See Next Page

INSTRUCTIONS

1. Preheat the grill over medium high heat. Spray grill with cooking oil spray.

2. Meanwhile, place chicken breast between sheets of plastic wrap and pound with a mallet for about ½-inch thick. Season chicken breast with olive oil, salt and pepper.

3. Grill chicken for 3-5 minutes per side or until cooked. Set aside and keep warm.

4. In a large bowl, whisk together vinegar, mustard and honey. Whisk in oil slowly. Season with salt and ground black pepper. Stir in fresh basil.

5. Chop grilled chicken and place in a bowl. Stir in barbecue sauce. Toss gently to combine.

6. Place lettuce in a large serving bowl together with chopped tomatoes, cucumber, zucchini, cheddar and red onion. Stir in dressing.

7. Serve salad, top with chicken barbecue.

8. Eat, Enjoy and Be Healthy!

BBQ Chicken Sandwich
With Balsamic Spinach

SERVINGS: 1 COOK TIME: 15 MINUTES

Nutritional Facts

Calories	Protein	Fat	Carbs	Dietary Fiber	Sugar
675	37g	35g	57g	7g	17g

INGREDIENTS

2 tbsp barbecue sauce

1 4 oz chicken breast or rotisserie chicken (skins removed)

1 cup baby spinach

½ cup carrots, shredded

2 tbsp slivered walnuts

2 tbsp balsamic vinaigrette

1 gluten free hamburger buns, toasted

INSTRUCTIONS

1. Brush or coat chicken breast with the barbecue sauce. Grill chicken breast until completely cooked. Alternatively, use rotisserie chicken to save time.

2. In a bowl, combine spinach, carrots, walnuts and balsamic vinaigrette. Toss to combine.

3. Fill toasted buns with chicken barbecue. Serve with salad.

4. Eat, Enjoy and Be Healthy!

Cranberry-
Orange Glazed
Turkey

SERVINGS: 4 COOK TIME: 15 MINUTES

Nutritional Facts

Calories	Protein	Fat	Carbs	Dietary Fiber	Sugar
285	30g	8g	18g	4g	12g

INGREDIENTS

1 tbsp grass fed butter

1 tbsp olive oil

8 (2-oz each) turkey cutlets

½ tsp Himalayan pink salt

¼ tsp freshly ground black pepper

¼ cup coconut flour or almond flour

1/2 cup fresh orange juice

2 tsp Dijon mustard

1/3 cup dried cranberries

INSTRUCTIONS

1. Melt butter and oil in a large skillet over low heat.

2. Meanwhile, season turkey cutlets with salt and pepper.

3. Place flour in a shallow plate. Roll turkey cutlets in flour, shaking off excess.

4. Increase the heat to medium-high and let the butter/oil turns golden brown. Add turkey cutlets and cook both sides until golden brown.

5. Transfer cooked cutlets to a plate and keep warm.

6. To the same skillet, add orange juice, mustard and cranberries. Scrape sides and bottom of pan to loosen browned bits. Bring to a boil.

7. Lower the heat and let the sauce simmer until it reduces to 2/3 cup, about 4-5 minutes.

8. Drizzle sauce over cutlets just before serving.

9. Eat, Enjoy and Be Healthy!

Turkey Meatballs

SERVINGS: 6 COOK TIME: 20-25 MINUTES

Nutritional Facts

Calories	Protein	Fat	Carbs	Dietary Fiber	Sugar
315	30g	16g	11g	1g	8g

INGREDIENTS

2 lbs ground turkey

2 eggs

3 celery stalks, diced

2 garlic cloves, chopped

1 yellow onion, diced

½ cup dried cranberries, coarsely chopped

1 tbsp herbs de Provence

1 tbsp olive oil

Himalayan pink salt

Ground black pepper

INSTRUCTIONS

1. Preheat oven to 400°F .

2. Heat olive oil in a skillet over medium high heat. Add diced onion and celery. Season to taste with salt and pepper. Sauté until vegetables are soft and slightly brown.

3. Add garlic and sauté until mixture starts to caramelize. Add cranberries and herbs de Provence. Mix well. Remove from heat and set aside to cool.

4. In a large bowl, combine ground turkey, eggs and cooled vegetable mixture. Form mixture into evenly sized meatballs, then arrange meatballs into a baking sheet.

5. Bake meatballs until completely cooked, about 20-25 minutes.

6. Eat, Enjoy and Be Healthy!

Turkey
Taco Burger

SERVINGS: 4 PREP TIME: 10 MINUTES COOK TIME: 10 MINUTES

Nutritional Facts

Calories	Protein	Fat	Carbs	Dietary Fiber	Sugar
625	42.5g	30g	46.5g	5g	2g

INGREDIENTS

1 ½ lb ground turkey

1 tbsp taco seasoning

1 cup tortilla chips, finely crushed

1 large egg, beaten

½ small yellow onion

4 slices white cheddar cheese

Topping suggestions

sour cream

salsa

guacamole

lettuce

tomato

Buns (gluten free)

INSTRUCTIONS

1. In a large bowl, combine ground turkey, taco seasoning, crushed tortilla chips, and beaten eggs.

2. Grate onion over the bowl to catch all the juice. Mix it all together until fully incorporated.

3. Divide and shape the mixture into four equal patties, pressing down the middle of each so they are slightly thinner in the middle.

4. Place patties on a sheet pan lined with foil and broil (4 to 5 inches away from heat) on high for about 6 minutes.

5. Flip to cook the other side for another 3 minutes.

6. Add cheese slices and cook until cheese is melted.

7. Place patties into each buns with your choice of garnish.

8. Serve immediately.

9. Eat, Enjoy and Be Healthy!

Ground Turkey
Taco Salad

SERVINGS: 5   COOK TIME: 20 MINUTES

Nutritional Facts

Calories	Protein	Fat	Carbs	Dietary Fiber	Sugar
235	31g	12g	25g	8g	5g

INGREDIENTS

1 ½ lbs ground turkey

1 medium onion, diced

1 (15 oz) can pinto beans, drained

1 tbsp taco seasoning

1 cup salsa

6 cups romaine lettuce, roughly chopped into bite sized pieces

Suggested Vegetable Toppings

Tomatoes

Carrots

Avocados

Peppers

Jalapeños

Other Suggested Toppings

Salsa

Low-fat cheese

Fat-free sour cream

INSTRUCTIONS

1. Heat skillet over medium heat and cook together ground turkey and onion until turkey is no longer pink and onion is soft.

2. Drain the sautéed mixture, then stir in beans, taco seasoning, and salsa.

3. Reduce the heat and let the mixture simmer for about 5 minutes

4. Divide lettuce onto five plates, top with cooked ground turkey.

5. Garnish with your own choice of suggested toppings.

6. For the dressing, use your favorite salsa or low fat salad dressing.

7. Eat, Enjoy and Be Healthy!

Turkey Chili

SERVINGS: 6   COOK TIME: 30 MINUTES

Nutritional Facts

Calories	Protein	Fat	Carbs	Dietary Fiber	Sugar
285	30g	13g	11g	3g	7g

INGREDIENTS

2 lbs ground turkey
2 zucchini, shredded
½ onion, shredded
1 can of kidney beans (light red)
2 (14-oz) cans of crushed tomatoes
1 tbsp chili
1 tsp cumin
1 tsp garlic salt
Himalayan pink salt
Ground pepper to taste
2 cups of water

INSTRUCTIONS

1. Heat oil over medium heat. Add ground turkey and cook until brown.

2. Stir in shredded zucchini and onion. Cook until onion is translucent.

3. Stir in kidney beans, crushed tomatoes, chili, cumin, garlic salt, Himalayan pink salt, ground pepper and water.

4. Reduce the heat and let the mixture simmer for about 20 minutes.

5. If the mixture becomes too thick, add water as necessary.

6. Eat, Enjoy and Be Healthy!

Curried Turkey Burgers With
Mango Slaw

SERVINGS: 6   PREP TIME: 5 MINUTES   COOK TIME: 20 MINUTES

Nutritional Facts

Calories	Protein	Fat	Carbs	Dietary Fiber	Sugar
265	30g	13g	16g	2.5g	13g

INGREDIENTS

For the Burger

2 lbs ground turkey

1 tbsp red curry paste

3 green onions, minced

Salt to taste

For the Mango Slaw

2 ripe mangoes, peeled and pitted, sliced into thin strips

2 red bell peppers, sliced into thin strips

1 English cucumber, slice into thin strips

3 green onions, minced

1 tsp lime zest

2 tbsp lime juice

1 tsp honey

2 tbsp fresh mint leaves, minced

½ tsp red curry paste

Salt to taste

Please See Next Page

INSTRUCTIONS

1. Preheat the oven to 400°F. Prepare a baking sheet and line with foil.

2. Combine turkey, curry paste, green onions and salt in a large mixing bowl.

3. Shape turkey mixture into patties and place in a roasting rack.

4. Bake patties for about 20 minutes or until cooked through.

5. Meanwhile, prepare the mango slaw by combining mangoes, cucumber, red bell pepper and green onion in a large mixing bowl.

6. Stir in lime zest, lime juice, honey, mint leaves, red curry paste and salt. Toss gently to combine.

7. Refrigerate mango slaw for about 15 minutes before using, for the flavours to blend.

8. Eat, Enjoy and Be Healthy!

Grilled
Lamb Chops

SERVINGS: 4   PREP TIME: 2 MINUTES   COOK TIME: 6 MINUTES

Nutritional Facts

Calories	Protein	Fat	Carbs	Dietary Fiber	Sugar
375	35g	26g	0.5g	0.5g	0g

INGREDIENTS

¾ tsp ground cinnamon

½ tsp freshly ground black pepper

¼ tsp ground all spice

¼ tsp ground cumin

1/8 tsp Himalayan pink salt

1/8 tsp ground red pepper

8 (4-ounce) lamb loin chops, trimmed (about
1-inch thick)

Coconut oil cooking spray

INSTRUCTIONS

1. Preheat the grill.

2. In a small bowl, combine ground cinnamon, ground black pepper, ground allspice, ground cumin, salt and ground red pepper. Mix well.

3. Rub lamb with the spiced mixture. Place lamb on a grill rack coated with cooking spray.

4. Grill lamb until desired degree of doneness is achieved, about 4 to 5 minutes per side for medium rare.

5. Serve with lime wedges, if desired.

6. Eat, Enjoy and Be Healthy!

Spicy
Grilled Lamb Kebabs

SERVINGS: 8   PREP TIME: 15 MINUTES   COOK TIME: 15 MINUTES

Nutritional Facts

Calories	Protein	Fat	Carbs	Dietary Fiber	Sugar
530	40g	40g	2g	0.5g	0.5g

INGREDIENTS

4 lbs boned leg of lamb, cut into 2cm cubes

For the marinade

1/3 cup of yogurt

½ cup of ginger

5 garlic cloves

½ tsp red chili powder, or to taste

1 tbsp vegetable oil

2 tsp red wine vinegar

1 tbsp garam masala

1 tbsp ground cumin

INSTRUCTIONS

1. In a shallow large bow, combine all ingredients for the marinade. Whisk until smooth. Season with salt and fresh ground pepper.

2. Add lamb cubes and combine thoroughly. Refrigerate overnight.

3. Before grilling, soak 8 wooden skewers in water. for at least 10 minutes.

4. Thread lamb onto the skewers, about 4 pieces each.

5. Grill lamb until charred on all sides and meat is well done.

6. Eat, Enjoy and Be Healthy!

Roast Lamb With
Red Currant Gravy

SERVINGS: 3   COOK TIME: 30 MINUTES

Nutritional Facts

Calories	Protein	Fat	Carbs	Dietary Fiber	Sugar
365	30g	17g	23g	3g	5g

INGREDIENTS

1/3 cup of yogurt.

½ cup of ginger

1 ¾ cups of new potatoes

1 cup of carrots, cut into big chunks

1 tbsp oil (plus extra oil for lamb)

1 sprig rosemary, leaves chopped

½ cup red wine

½ cup lamb stock

Red currant jelly

INSTRUCTIONS

1. Preheat the oven to 425°F.

2. In a large bowl, combine potatoes, carrots, oil and chopped rosemary. Toss everything to combine. Season with salt and pepper.

3. Spread the potatoes and carrots onto a baking tray and roast until tender, about 15 minutes

4. To cook the gravy, pour wine and stock into a small saucepan and bring to a boil.

5. When the liquid has reduced by two-thirds, stir in red currant jelly. Mix well, then remove from heat and set aside to keep warm.

6. Rub the lamb with oil. Season with salt and pepper.

7. Place lamb on top of the vegetables. Roast for 8 to 10 minutes, turning once halfway during roasting.

8. Serve roasted lamb with red currant gravy and a side dish of green vegetables.

9. Eat, Enjoy and Be Healthy!

Lamb Chops With
Arugula Pesto

SERVINGS: 4   PREP TIME: 3 MINUTES   COOK TIME: 10 MINUTES

Nutritional Facts

Calories	Protein	Fat	Carbs	Dietary Fiber	Sugar
450	36.5g	31.5g	5g	2g	1g

INGREDIENTS

8 (4-ounce) lean lamb loin chops, trimmed

½ tsp salt, divided

½ tsp freshly ground black pepper, divided

Coconut oil spray

1 lemon

1 tbsp pine nuts, toasted

2 garlic cloves

4 cups baby arugula leaves

2 tsp olive oil

2 tbsp water

INSTRUCTIONS

1. Preheat the broiler.

2. Season lamb with ¼ tsp salt and ¼ tsp ground pepper.

3. Place lamb evenly in a single layer on a broiler pan coated with cooking spray. Broil for 5 to 6 minutes on each side.

4. Meanwhile, grate 1 tsp lemon rind and squeeze juice from lemon to measure 2 tsp.

5. Process pine nuts and garlic in a food processor until coarsely chopped.

6. Add lemon rind, lemon juice, arugula, oil, 2 tbsp water, ¼ tsp salt, and ¼ tsp ground pepper to the food processor and process mixture until smooth.

7. Serve lamb with arugula pesto.

8. Eat, Enjoy and Be Healthy!

Thyme
Pork Tenderloin

SERVINGS: 3 COOK TIME: 30 MINUTES

Nutritional Facts

Calories	Protein	Fat	Carbs	Dietary Fiber	Sugar
240	34g	9g	1.5g	1g	0.5g

INGREDIENTS

1 tsp dried thyme

1 tsp instant onion flakes

1 slice day old bread (gluten free)

2 large egg whites, beaten

1 lb pork tenderloin, trimmed

¼ tsp Himalayan pink salt

¼ tsp fresh ground black pepper

Coconut oil cooking spray

INSTRUCTIONS

1. Preheat the oven to 400°F degrees. Spray a broiler pan with cooking oil spray.

2. In a food processor, combine thyme, onion and bread. Pulse until fine bread crumbs is achieved, you should have about 1/3 cup of fine bread crumbs.

3. Place bread crumbs in a shallow plate and season pork with a dash of salt and pepper.

4. Dip pork in egg whites, and then dredge in bread crumbs mixture.

5. Arrange pork in a broiler pan and bake for about 20 minutes. Remove from the oven and let it rest for 5 minutes.

6. Slice grilled pork into ¼-inch thick slices.

7. Eat, Enjoy and Be Healthy!

Pork and Beans

SERVINGS: 5   COOK TIME: 25 MINUTES

Nutritional Facts

Calories	Protein	Fat	Carbs	Dietary Fiber	Sugar
350	40g	15g	13g	5g	2g

INGREDIENTS

2 tbsp olive oil

8 pork cutlets (about 4 oz each), each pounded to about ¼ inch thick

1 large yellow bell pepper, thinly sliced

1 large red bell pepper, thinly sliced

2 shallots (about 1 ounce), thinly sliced

1 cup navy beans, rinsed

½ cup pitted olives, halved

½ cup fresh parsley, chopped

1 tbsp red wine vinegar

Himalayan pink salt, to taste

Ground black pepper to taste

INSTRUCTIONS

1. Heat half of oil in a large skillet over medium heat.

2. Meanwhile, season pork with salt and pepper.

3. Brown pork cutlets on each side, then transfer to a plate.

4. Use a separate skillet to heat the remaining oil. Add bell peppers, shallots, ½ tsp of salt and ¼ tsp fresh ground black pepper. Cook, stirring frequently until vegetables are soft, about 5 minutes.

5. Add navy beans, olives, fresh parsley and vinegar. Toss gently to combine.

6. Serve pork cutlets top with vegetable mixture.

7. Eat, Enjoy and Be Healthy!

Pork Tenderloin With
Mustard And
Cornflakes

SERVINGS: 4   PREP TIME: 5 MINUTES   COOK TIME: 15 MINUTES

Nutritional Facts

Calories	Protein	Fat	Carbs	Dietary Fiber	Sugar
295	37g	11g	11g	1g	2g

INGREDIENTS

1 ½ lbs pork tenderloin, butterflied

3 tbsp whole grain mustard or Dijon mustard

1 cup cornflakes

INSTRUCTIONS

1. Place cornflakes in a food processor and process until the texture becomes coarse crumbs. Place in a shallow plate.

2. Rub pork tenderloin with mustard evenly, then roll in cornflakes.

3. Grill or pan-fry for approximately 15 minutes. Cooking time varies depending on the thickness of meat.

4. Eat, Enjoy and Be Healthy!

Pork Cutlets With Peppers And Cannellini Beans

SERVINGS: 4   COOK TIME: 25 MINUTES

Nutritional Facts

Calories	Protein	Fat	Carbs	Dietary Fiber	Sugar
400	41g	17g	20g	7.5g	2g

INGREDIENTS

2 tbsp olive oil

8 pork cutlets (about 1 ½ lbs), pounded to ¼-inch thick

Kosher salt

Fresh ground black pepper

2 medium bell peppers, thinly sliced

2 large shallots, thinly sliced

1 (15.5-oz) can cannellini beans, rinsed

½ cup pitted kalamata olives, halved

½ cup fresh flat-leaf parsley leaves

1 tbsp red wine vinegar

INSTRUCTIONS

1. Season pork with salt and pepper. Set aside.

2. Heat a large skillet over medium heat. Add oil.

3. Brown pork the pork, about 2 to 3 minutes per side. Transfer in a plate and set aside.

4. In another large skillet, heat the remaining oil.

5. Sauté bell peppers, shallots, ½ teaspoon salt, and ¼ teaspoon black pepper. Cook, stirring frequently until vegetables softened, about 5 to 7 minutes.

6. Stir in cannellini beans, olives, parsley, and vinegar. Toss to combine.

7. Serve pork topped with the vegetable mixture.

8. Eat, Enjoy and Be Healthy!

Pork Tenderloin With
Figs & Onion

SERVINGS: 4   PREP TIME: 4 MINUTES   COOK TIME: 19 MINUTES

Nutritional Facts

Calories	Protein	Fat	Carbs	Dietary Fiber	Sugar
250	32g	4.5g	19g	3g	11g

INGREDIENTS

1 ½ lbs pork tenderloin, trimmed

¼ tsp salt

¼ tsp ground black pepper

Cooking spray

8 dried Mission figs, coarsely chopped

2 tbsp balsamic vinegar

2 tbsp water

1 tbsp coconut aminos

1 (8-oz) container refrigerated onion, pre-chopped

INSTRUCTIONS

1. Preheat the oven to 425°F.

2. Season pork with salt and ground pepper. Spray with cooking oil spray.

3. Heat skillet over medium heat. Spray with cooking oil spray.

4. Brown pork on both sides, about 4 to 5 minutes on each side. Transfer cooked pork on a baking pan.

5. In a small bowl, combine vinegar, 2 tbsp of water and coconut aminos.

6. Wipe the skillet, then add figs, onion and vinegar mixture, stirring to loosen browned bits that sticks to the bottom and sides.

7. Bake pork, uncovered for 15 minutes.

8. Stir in onion mixture, cover pan loosely with foil and let it cool for 5 minutes before slicing.

9. Eat, Enjoy and Be Healthy!

Herbed Butter Sauce

SERVINGS: 4   PREP TIME: 10 MINUTES   COOK TIME: 10 MINUTES

Nutritional Facts

Calories	Protein	Fat	Carbs	Dietary Fiber	Sugar
430	35g	31.5g	1g	0.5g	0.5g

INGREDIENTS

4 pork loin rib chops

2 tsp kosher salt

1 tsp freshly ground black pepper

2 tbsp unsalted butter

2 tbsp shallots, finely chopped

¼ cup dry white wine

2 tsp Italian flat-leaf parsley, chopped

INSTRUCTIONS

1. Season pork chops with ½ tsp sugar, ¼ tsp salt, and 1/8 tsp pepper on both sides. Refrigerate for 1 to 2 hours or overnight.

2. When ready to cook, preheat the oven to 450° F.

3. Heat an oven-proofs skillet over medium heat. Add 2 tbsp of butter.

4. Sear pork chops quickly, about 1 minute per side, or until you get a nice crispy crust on the outside without burning the chops. Be careful not to burn them!

5. When the chops are nicely seared on both sides, place the skillet right into the oven. Cook for about 5 minutes.

6. When the pork reaches 140°F, transfer to a cutting board and let rest for at least 10 minutes before cutting into thin slices.

7. Serve pan-seared pork chops with herb-butter sauce.

8. Eat, Enjoy and Be Healthy!

Cuban Burger

SERVINGS: 6   PREP TIME: 10 MINUTES   COOK TIME: 15 MINUTES

Nutritional Facts

Calories	Protein	Fat	Carbs	Dietary Fiber	Sugar
540	33g	34g	29g	2g	1g

INGREDIENTS

For the 'Bun"

3 green plantains

Coconut oil

Salt to taste

For the 'Burger'

2 pounds ground pork

1 tbsp onion powder

1 tbsp dried oregano

2 tsp granulated garlic

1 tbsp lime juice

Salt to taste

For the 'Toppings'

Shaved Deli ham

Yellow mustard

Honey

Dill Pickles

Please See Next Page

INSTRUCTIONS

1. For the buns, peel the plantains and slice into 2-inch-thick rounds.

2. Bring a large pot of water to a boil. Boil plantain rounds until soft, about 5 minutes.

3. Remove the plantains and smash flat with the back of a plate. If the plantain sticks to the plate, scrape it off with a spatula. Seasoned with salt.

4. In a skillet, melt a few tablespoons of coconut oil over medium-high heat. Fry flattened plantains until brown and crispy, about 3 minutes per side.

5. For the burger, place all ingredients in a bowl. Use your hands to mix everything together thoroughly. Form the burgers roughly the same size as the plantain buns.

6. Cook the burgers in skillet, adding more oil if needed, about 5 minutes per side.

7. To assemble, place a bun on a plate, top with a burger patty, plus any desired toppings, and cap off with another platain bun.

8. Serve immediately.

Spinach Salad with Salmon

Nectarines and Pecans

SERVINGS: 2 COOK TIME: 15 minutes

Nutritional Facts

Calories	Protein	Fat	Carbs	Dietary Fiber	Sugar
524	31g	39g	32g	17g	14g

INGREDIENTS

2 1/2 cups of baby spinach leaves

½ ripe avocado, chopped into pieces

½ ripe nectarine, chopped into pieces

½ cup cherry tomatoes, chopped into pieces

1/3 cup raw pecans

8oz fresh wild salmon with skin

1 ½ tsp. avocado oil

Vinaigrette

3 tsp fresh lemon juice

3 tsp walnut oil

¼ tsp Dijon-style mustard

A dash of ground black pepper

INSTRUCTIONS

1. Preheat the oven to 400° degrees.

2. Place a cast iron pan over medium high heat. When hot, add avocado oil.

3. Sear salmon skin side down in the center of the pan for about 2-3 minutes.

4. Place cast iron pan inside the oven and continue cooking the salmon until it is firm to the touch, about 2-4 minutes or depending on thickness.

5. Meanwhile, in a bowl, assemble the spinach, chopped avocado, nectarines and tomatoes and pecans.

6. In a separate small bowl, combine freshly squeezed lemon juice with the Dijon-style mustard.Whisk gently, then slowly add walnut oil, while whisking continuously until the dressing emulsified.

7. Season with a dash of freshly ground pepper.

8. To serve, drizzle the vinaigrette dressing over the spinach salad, top with cooked salmon.

9. Eat, Enjoy and Be Healthy!

Wild Salmon Curry with Tomatoes

SERVINGS: 4 COOK TIME: 20 MINUTES

Nutritional Facts

Calories	Protein	Fat	Carbs	Dietary Fiber	Sugar
315	30g	14g	17g	3g	4g

INGREDIENTS

1 cup long grain white rice

4 cups grape tomatoes

1 tbsp olive oil

Himalayan pink salt

Ground black pepper

1 ½ lbs wild salmon fillets

2 tsp curry powder

¼ cup fresh basil, torn into pieces

INSTRUCTIONS

1. Heat the oven to 400°F.

2. Cook rice according to package instructions.

3. In a bowl, combine tomatoes, oil, ¼ tsp salt and ¼ tsp ground black pepper. Toss gently to combine.

4. Transfer the tomato mixture into a rimmed baking sheet. Spread evenly.

5. Arrange salmon fillet over tomato mixture. Sprinkle curry powder, ½ tsp salt and ¼ tsp ground black pepper.

6. Roast salmon for about 18 minutes or until fish flakes easily when prick with fork.

7. Serve over rice with a garnish of torn fresh basil.

8. Eat, Enjoy and Be Healthy!

Salmon With
Mint Dressing

SERVINGS: 6   PREP TIME: 10 MINUTES   COOK TIME: 10 MINUTES

Nutritional Facts

Calories	Protein	Fat	Carbs	Dietary Fiber	Sugar
545	37g	26g	40g	6g	7g

INGREDIENTS

3 cups of potatoes, thickly sliced

3 cups of frozen peas and beans

3 tbsp olive oil

Zest and juice of 1 lemon

Small pack mint, leaves only

4 salmon fillets (about 4-oz each)

4 cups grate tomatoes (halved)

INSTRUCTIONS

1. Preheat over to 450°F.

2. Boil potatoes with enough water to cover for 4 minutes.

3. Add in peas and beans. Bring to a boil, then cook for another 3 minutes or until the potatoes and beans are tender.

4. Use a blender to whizz the olive oil, lemon zest and juice and mint to make a dressing.

5. Put salmon in an oven safe dish and cover with dressing.

6. Bake salmon at 450°F for 12-15 minutes.

7. Drain the cooked vegetables and mix with the hot dressing and cooking juices from the fish.

8. Serve fish on top of the vegetables.

9. Eat, Enjoy and Be Healthy!

Lemon
Sriracha Salmon

SERVINGS: 3   COOK TIME: 20 MINUTES

Nutritional Facts

Calories	Protein	Fat	Carbs	Dietary Fiber	Sugar
360	30g	24g	6g	0g	3g

INGREDIENTS

1 lb of salmon, cut into 3 filets

4 tbsp butter

Zest of 1 lemon

Juice of 2 lemons

4 tbsp Sriracha sauce

4 cloves of garlic

Salt and pepper to taste

3 cups of potatoes

3 cups of frozen peas

INSTRUCTIONS

1. Preheat over to 450°F.

2. Melt butter in a skillet over medium heat.

3. Sauté the garlic until fragrant, about 1 minute.

4. Stir in salmon filets, lemon juice, lemon zest and Sriracha sauce.

5. Bake salmon at 450°F for 12-15 minutes.

6. Eat, Enjoy and Be Healthy!

Roasted Spaghetti Squash With Garlic Shrimp

SERVINGS: 4   COOK TIME: 25 MINUTES

Nutritional Facts

Calories	Protein	Fat	Carbs	Dietary Fiber	Sugar
350	36g	16.5g	14g	3g	5g

INGREDIENTS

1 ½ lbs spaghetti squash, halved lengthwise and seeded

2 tbsp extra-virgin olive oil

1 tbsp garlic, minced

1 tsp ground coriander

1 tsp ground cumin

½ tsp salt, divided

¼ tsp cayenne pepper

1/3 cup dry white wine

1½ lbs raw shrimp, peeled and deveined (leaving the tails intact)

1 tbsp lemon juice

¼ cup fresh cilantro, chopped

2 tbsp unsalted butter, melted

¼ tsp ground pepper

Lemon wedges for serving

Please See Next Page

INSTRUCTIONS

1. Place squash in a microwave safe dish, cut side down with 2 tbsp of water. Microwave on High, uncovered for about 10 minutes or until squash are soft.

2. Alternatively, place squash on a rimmed baking sheet and bake at 400°F oven for 40 to 50 minutes.

3. Sauté garlic with coriander, cumin and ¼ tsp of salt over medium heat for 30 seconds.

4. Pour in wine. Lower the heat and bring to a slow simmer.

5. Add shrimp and cook, stirring, until the shrimp are pink, about 3 to 4 minutes. Remove from heat. Stir in lemon juice.

6. Meanwhile, scrape the squash flesh and place in a medium bowl.

7. Stir in cilantro, butter, pepper and the remaining ¼ tsp salt. Stir to combine.

8. Serve shrimp over the spaghetti squash with a garnish of lemon wedge on the side.

9. Eat, Enjoy and Be Healthy!

Asian Pepper
Shrimp with Cilantro

SERVINGS: 3 COOK TIME: 15 minutes

Nutritional Facts

Calories	Protein	Fat	Carbs	Dietary Fiber	Sugar
275	31g	16g	5g	0.5g	0.5g

INGREDIENTS

3 tbsp coconut oil

4 cloves garlic, crushed

1 ½ lb raw shrimp, peeled with tails on

1 tbsp coconut aminos

1 tbsp fish sauce

¾ tsp ground black pepper

¼ cup fresh cilantro, chopped

INSTRUCTIONS

1. Melt coconut oil in a skillet over low heat. Add crushed garlic and sauté for about 3 minutes, or until garlic soften.

2. Add shrimp. Sauté until shrimp turns pink, around 5 minutes or depending how large your shrimps are.

3. Stir in coconut aminos, fish sauce and ground black pepper. Sauté for 1 minute.

4. Arrange shrimps on a serving plate.

5. Heat the remaining liquid from the skillet and pour this over shrimp.

6. Serve shrimp with a sprinkle of chopped cilantro.

7. Eat, Enjoy and Be Healthy!

Cheesy Shrimps And Grits

SERVINGS: 4   COOK TIME: 25 MINUTES

Nutritional Facts

Calories	Protein	Fat	Carbs	Dietary Fiber	Sugar
375	32g	14g	30g	2g	0.5g

INGREDIENTS

1 (14-oz) can chicken broth (low sodium)

1 ½ cups water

1 cup quick grits

½ tsp freshly ground black pepper, divided

1 cup Cheddar cheese

1 ½ lbs raw shrimp, peeled and deveined

1 bunch scallions, cut into 1-inch pieces

1 tbsp extra-virgin olive oil

¼ tsp garlic powder

1/8 tsp salt

INSTRUCTIONS

1. Preheat the broiler. Place rack in upper third of oven.

2. Combine water and chicken broth in a large saucepan and bring to a boil over medium heat. Stir in grits and half of the ground black pepper.

3. Lower the heat to medium low, cover the pan and cook, stirring frequently until the mixture is thick, about 5 to 7 minutes.

4. Remove from heat and stir in cheese. Cover to keep warm.

5. In a medium bowl, combine shrimp, scallions, oil, garlic powder, remaining half of ground black pepper and salt. Stir to combine.

6. Spread mixture evenly on a rimmed baking sheet.

7. Broil until shrimp are pink and just cooked through, 5 to 6 minutes.

8. Serve cheesy shrimp and grits with scallions.

9. Eat, Enjoy and Be Healthy!

Curried Shrimp With Sugar Snap Peas

SERVINGS: 4   COOK TIME: 25 MINUTES

Nutritional Facts

Calories	Protein	Fat	Carbs	Dietary Fiber	Sugar
320	39g	14g	9g	3g	4.5g

INGREDIENTS

2 tbsp olive oil

2 tbsp Madras curry powder

1 ½ lbs raw shrimp, peeled and deveined

1 lb sugar snap peas, trimmed

1 cup "lite" coconut milk

¼ cup lemon juice

½ tsp salt

INSTRUCTIONS

1. Heat a large skillet over medium heat. Add oil.

2. When hot, add curry powder and cook, stirring, until fragrant, 1 to 2 minutes.

3. Stir in shrimp and sugar snap peas. Cook for about 4 minutes or until shrimp are almost cooked.

4. Pour in coconut milk.

5. Stir in lemon juice and salt and bring to a boil.

6. Continue cooking for another 2 minutes or until shrimp are cooked completely.

7. Eat, Enjoy and Be Healthy!

Spicy Grilled
Shrimp

SERVINGS: 5   PREP TIME: 10 MINUTES   COOK TIME: 20 MINUTES

Nutritional Facts

Calories	Protein	Fat	Carbs	Dietary Fiber	Sugar
315	37g	16g	5g	0.5g	4.5g

INGREDIENTS

2 ¼ lbs jumbo shrimp, peeled (leaving the tails intact)

¾ cup Honeyed Lemon-Dijon Vinaigrette, divided

½ tsp crushed red pepper

¼ tsp salt

¼ tsp coarsely ground black pepper

Cooking oil spray

Lemon wedges

INSTRUCTIONS

1. 2 ¼ lbs jumbo shrimp, peeled (leaving the tails intact)

2. ¾ cup Honeyed Lemon-Dijon Vinaigrette, divided

3. ½ tsp crushed red pepper

4. ¼ tsp salt

5. ¼ tsp coarsely ground black pepper

6. Cooking oil spray

7. Lemon wedges

Lemon Pepper
Shrimp

SERVINGS: 3   PREP TIME: 5 MINUTES   COOK TIME: 10 MINUTES

Nutritional Facts

Calories	Protein	Fat	Carbs	Dietary Fiber	Sugar
265	40g	12g	2g	0g	0.5g

INGREDIENTS

2 lbs large shrimp, peeled and deveined

1 organic lemon, juiced and zested

½ tsp black pepper, freshly ground

½ tsp salt, or as needed

1 tbsp extra virgin olive oil

2 tbsp fresh parsley, chopped

INSTRUCTIONS

1. In a large bowl, combine shrimp, lemon juice and lemon zest. Season to taste with salt and black pepper. Toss to combine.

2. Heat skillet over medium heat. Add olive oil. Fry shrimp for about 5 to 6 minutes or until cooked through.

3. Remove shrimp from heat, then stir in chopped parsley. Season with salt and pepper.

4. Serve with extra parsley on top and lemon wedges on the sides.

5. Eat, Enjoy and Be Healthy!

Tuna Salad

SERVINGS: 2 PREP TIME: 10 MINUTES

Nutritional Facts

Calories	Protein	Fat	Carbs	Dietary Fiber	Sugar
220	33.5g	2.5g	16g	2.5g	8.5g

INGREDIENTS

1 large sweet onion, chopped

2 large tomatoes, chopped

1 bunch of fresh cilantro, chopped

1 large can of light tuna, drained

Juice from 1 lime

INSTRUCTIONS

1. Flake tuna into bite-sized pieces. Set aside.

2. Place chopped onion in a large bowl and add a tbsp of salt and enough water to cover the onions. This process will help to remove the bitter aftertaste of the onion.

3. Set aside for about 30 minutes.

4. Add in tomatoes and cilantro to the onion, then squeeze the lemon juice over the vegetables.

5. Stir in tuna. Toss gently to combine.

6. Eat, Enjoy and Be Healthy!

Fennel And Bean Salad

SERVINGS: 2   PREP TIME: 10 MINUTES

Nutritional Facts

Calories	Protein	Fat	Carbs	Dietary Fiber	Sugar
460	37.5g	17g	38.5g	14g	2g

INGREDIENTS

1 large can of solid white albacore tuna, drained

Zest of half lemon

1 tbsp lemon juice

1 tsp whole grain mustard

1 tbsp extra virgin olive oil

15oz can cannellini beans, drained and rinsed

Small bunch of dill, chopped roughly

Small bunch of fresh parsley, chopped

INSTRUCTIONS

1. To prepare the dressing, combine lemon zest, lemon juice, mustard, oil, and a dash of seasonings in a jar. Shake the jar until the mixture is well combine.

2. Place beans into a bowl and toss with the dressings.

3. Add in herbs, fennel, cucumber and flaked tuna.

4. Place salad into a serving plates with a garnish of pumpkin seeds.

5. Eat, Enjoy and Be Healthy!

Tuna and, Parsley Pesto Sauce

SERVINGS: 4   PREP TIME: 10 MINUTES

Nutritional Facts

Calories	Protein	Fat	Carbs	Dietary Fiber	Sugar
560	30g	12g	83g	6g	4g

INGREDIENTS

2 cups brown rice pasta, dried

½ cup frozen green beans

1 cup cherry tomatoes, halved

1 cup of fresh parsley, roughly chopped

4 cans light albacore tuna in sunflower oil, drained

Water, drained

Zest and juice of 1 lemon

INSTRUCTIONS

1. Cook pasta according to package instructions. During the last 3 minutes of cooking time, add green beans and cherry tomatoes. Drain. Reserve a mug of the cooking water.

2. Meanwhile, in a food processor, combine fresh parsley, 3 tbsp of oil from tuna, lemon zest, lemon juice and the reserved cooking water. Add a dash of seasonings. Process until smooth.

3. Bring the cooked pasta back to the skillet with the vegetables. Stir in pesto, tuna and sour cream or cream cheese. Stir gently while still hot.

4. Eat, Enjoy and be Healthy!!

Pan Seared
Tuna Steaks

SERVINGS: 2   PREP TIME: 5 MINUTES   COOK TIME: 12 MINUTES

Nutritional Facts

Calories	Protein	Fat	Carbs	Dietary Fiber	Sugar
390	33g	19g	22g	9g	0g

INGREDIENTS

2 pieces ahi tuna steaks (each about 4 oz)

1 tsp Himalayan sea salt

¼ tsp cayenne pepper

½ tbsp butter (grass fed)

2 tbsp olive oil

1 tsp whole peppercorns

INSTRUCTIONS

1. Season tuna steaks with salt and cayenne pepper.

2. In a skillet, melt olive oil and butter over medium high heat. Add peppercorns and sauté until they pop up, about 4-5 minutes.

3. Place tuna steaks in skillet and cook for about 1 ½ minutes per side (for medium rare), or until you achieved your desired doneness.

4. Eat, Enjoy and Be Happy!

Tuna Steaks
Moroccan-Style

SERVINGS: 5 PREP TIME: 10 MINUTES

Nutritional Facts

Calories	Protein	Fat	Carbs	Dietary Fiber	Sugar
610	45g	47g	1g	0g	0g

INGREDIENTS

1/8 cup pack fresh coriander (leaves and stalks)

3 garlic cloves

½ tsp ground paprika

½ tsp ground cumin

½ tsp chili powder

1 tbsp lemon juice

2/3 cup extra virgin olive oil

4 tuna steaks (6 oz each)

INSTRUCTIONS

1. In a blender, combine fresh coriander, garlic, spices and lemon juice. Blitz to a smooth puree, adding olive oil slowly while the motor is running.

2. Blend until sauce is smooth and thick. Set aside.

3. Place tuna steaks in a bowl and cover with 2/3 of the sauce. Cover bowl with cling wrap. Refrigerate for about 20 minutes up to 4 hours.

4. Remove tuna from the sauce and season with salt and pepper. Grill tuna for about 2 minutes per side. Grilling time varies according to the thickness of fish.

5. Transfer tuna to a serving plate and drizzle with the remaining sauce.

6. Serve alongside new potatoes, for a Moroccan twist.

7. Eat, Enjoy and Be Healthy!

Tuna And
Lemon Pasta

SERVINGS: 4 PREP TIME: 5 MINUTES COOK TIME: 10 MINUTES

Nutritional Facts

Calories	Protein	Fat	Carbs	Dietary Fiber	Sugar
505	30g	12g	69g	6g	5g

INGREDIENTS

12oz gluten free spaghetti spaghetti pasta

4 cups broccoli, cut into small florets

2 tbsp shallots, finely chopped

¾ cup pitted green olives, halved

1 (7oz) can tuna in oil

Zest and juice of 1 lemon

1 tbsp olive oil, plus extra for drizzling

INSTRUCTIONS

1. Boil the spaghetti pasta according to package instructions. During the last 3 minutes of cooking time, add broccoli florets and cooked until tender. Drain.

2. Meanwhile, in a large bowl, combine shallots, olives, capers, tuna, lemon zest and lemon juice. Add cooked broccoli and pasta. Toss to combine.

3. Stir in olive oil and season generously with ground black pepper.

4. Serve with a drizzle of more olive oil.

5. Eat, Enjoy and Be Healthy!

Steamed Mussels

SERVINGS: 5 PREP TIME: 10 MINUTES COOK TIME: 13 MINUTES

Nutritional Facts

Calories	Protein	Fat	Carbs	Dietary Fiber	Sugar
370	44g	14g	16g	0g	1g

INGREDIENTS

1 tbsp extra virgin olive oil

4 cloves garlic, chopped

½ cup fresh basil, chopped

¼ cup white wine

1 cup vegetable broth

2 tbsp butter (grass fed)

4 lbs mussels (or use fresh clams)

Ground black pepper, to taste

Fresh basil (for garnish)

INSTRUCTIONS

1. Heat oil in a large stock pot over medium heat. Sauté garlic for 1 minute, then add chopped basil, wine, broth and butter. Bring to a boil.

2. When boiling, add clams and mussels, cover the pot and simmer for 5 minutes.

3. Stir. Cook until all mussels are open.

4. Remove mussels from the stockpot and divide into 4 pasta bowls. Season with salt and pepper.

5. Pour hot broth over mussels.

6. Serve warm with a garnish of fresh basil.

7. Eat, Enjoy and Be Healthy!

Asian Flounder Fillet

SERVINGS: 4 COOK TIME: 5-10 MINUTES

Nutritional Facts

Calories	Protein	Fat	Carbs	Dietary Fiber	Sugar
161	32g	4g	5g	1g	2g

INGREDIENTS

8 stalks green onions

¼ cup fresh cilantro, minced

1 tbsp fresh ginger, minced

2 tsp dark sesame oil, divided

4 (6 oz) flounder fillets, skins removed

2 tsp rice vinegar

2 tsp coconut aminos

1/8 tsp Himalayan pink salt

4 lemon slices

INSTRUCTIONS

1. Preheat oven to 425°F degrees.

2. Cut green onion (green parts) into 1-inch long, just enough to make ¼ cup. Cut white parts of green onion into 2-inch long.

3. In a bowl, combine cilantro, ginger and 1 tsp of oil. Mix well. Pour this mixture into a 9-oven safe pan.

4. Fold flounder fillet in half crosswise, the arrange fish on pan with the thinnest portions facing towards center of the pan.

5. Arrange half of the green onion slices between each fillet.

6. In a separate bowl, combine half of the remaining green onion, 1 tsp oil, coconut aminos, vinegar and salt. Whisk well. Pour over fish.

7. Bake flounder for 10-15 minutes or until flaky.

8. Serve fish fillet with a garnish of lemon slices.

9. Eat, Enjoy and Be Healthy!

Poached Bass
Over Frisee Salad

SERVINGS: 4   COOK TIME: 15 MINUTES

Nutritional Facts

Calories	Protein	Fat	Carbs	Dietary Fiber	Sugar
640	35g	46g	21g	1.5g	1.5g

INGREDIENTS

8 boneless bass fillets

1 shallot, sliced

6 sprigs fresh thyme

6 sprigs fresh parsley

1 tbsp mustard seeds

½ cup + 3 tbsp olive oil

Himalayan pink salt

Ground black pepper

1 head frisee (about 1 cup)

1 tbsp white wine vinegar

4 gluten free bread slices, toasted

INSTRUCTIONS

1. In a large skillet, combine sliced shallot, thyme, parsley, mustard seeds, ½ cup of oil, 1 cup water, ½ tsp salt and ¼ tsp ground black pepper. Bring to a slow simmer.

2. Add bass fillets, cover and cook until fish turns opaque in color, about 10-12 minutes.

3. Meanwhile, in a large bowl, combine the frisee, vinegar, remaining oil. ½ tsp salt and ¼ tsp ground black pepper. Toss gently to combine.

4. Serve poached fish over frisee and toasted bread.

5. Eat, Enjoy and Be Healthy!

Mahi-Mahi With
Macadamia Nut Crust

SERVINGS: 3   PREP TIME: 15 MINUTES   COOK TIME: 10 MINUTES

Nutritional Facts

Calories	Protein	Fat	Carbs	Dietary Fiber	Sugar
460	41g	35g	49g	4g	33g

INGREDIENTS

1 lb mahi-mahi fillets

1 ½ cups corn flakes

1 cup macadamia nuts

(may substitute pecans or walnuts)

2 tbsp fresh parsley, chopped

Himalayan salt

Gground black pepper

Cooking spray, for baking pan

Honey Glaze

1/3 cup honey

1/3 cup coconut aminos

2 tsp dry mustard

INSTRUCTIONS

1. Preheat the oven to 350°F.

2. Pulse macadamia nuts in a blender or food processor.

3. Add cornflakes and pulse again until both are coarsely chopped.

4. Spread macadamia/cornflakes mixture on a shallow plate and toss with chopped parsley, salt and pepper.

5. Roll fish fillet in the ground mixture, pressing gently for the breading to stick to the fish.

6. Place breaded fish on an oiled baking pan, 1-inch apart. Bake for 10 minutes or until fish is done.

7. Meanwhile, combine honey, coconut aminos and dry mustard in a small bowl. Mix well.

8. Serve mahi-mahi over plain rice. Drizzle honey glaze over the top.

9. Eat, Enjoy and Be Healthy!

Grilled Mahi-Mahi With
Spicy Carribean Sauce

SERVINGS: 2   PREP TIME: 5 MINUTES   COOK TIME: 15 MINUTES

Nutritional Facts

Calories	Protein	Fat	Carbs	Dietary Fiber	Sugar
255	44g	2g	14.5g	1.5g	0.5g

INGREDIENTS

2 (8-oz) mahi-mahi fillets

½ cup sour cream (fat-free)

2 tbsp fresh lime juice

2 tbsp fresh cilantro, chopped

1 jalapeno, seeded and chopped

INSTRUCTIONS

1. Season mahi-mahi with salt and pepper.
2. Meanwhile, preheat the grill. Cover with foil and spray with cooking oil spray.
3. Grill fish for about 5 to 7 minutes on each side.
4. In the food processor, combine sour cream, lime juice, fresh cilantro and jalapeno. Process on medium speed until mixture has a creamy consistency.
5. Serve grilled mahi-mahi with a drizzle of Caribbean sauce on top.
6. Eat, Enjoy and Be Healthy!

Sesame Seed
Crusted Snapper

SERVINGS 4 PREP TIME: 10 MINUTES COOK TIME: 10 MINUTES

Nutritional Facts

Calories	Protein	Fat	Carbs	Dietary Fiber	Sugar
310	36g	17g	3g	1g	0g

INGREDIENTS

4 red snapper fillet, skinned

4 tbsp sesame seeds

Himalayan pink salt, to taste

Freshly cracked black pepper, to taste

4 tbsp butter (grass fed)

INSTRUCTIONS

1. Season red snapper lightly with salt and ground black pepper.

2. Lay seasoned fish on the bed of sesame seeds, pressing down to ensure an even coating. Flip over to coat the other side.

3. Heat a frying pan over medium heat. Melt butter.

4. Pan-fry fish for about 3 to 4 minutes on each side or until golden in color.

5. Let the fish rest for a few minutes then serve.

6. Eat, Enjoy and Be Healthy!

Thank You for using the Shredded Chef Cookbook to make 101 meals that are not only super healthy but great tasting too!

I hope you enjoyed the recipes and you found them as easy to make as I do.

If you are looking for someone to help you reach your health and fitness goals I would be happy to help you change your life. I offer online coaching, 1 on 1 training, and nutrition coaching to help you look and feel your absolute best. Connect with me below for a complimentary assessment and review of your goals.

If you would like to work with Mike please email him at Mike@IronForkFitness.com

Mike Kneuer – CPT, CES, FNS, FAS, Pro Physique Athlete

Connect with Mike

Mike@ProjectShredded.com
Facebook.com/MikeKneuer82
Instagram.com/WhatMikeEats
Twitter.com/WhatMikeEats
Linkedin.com/in/MikeKneuer
Youtube.com/c/MikeKneuer82
Google.com/+MikeKneuer82

CPSIA information can be obtained
at www.ICGtesting.com
Printed in the USA
LVHW070228091122
732722LV00002B/12

9 781329 712867